A Short History
of the
U.S. WORKING CLASS

A Short History
of the
U.S. WORKING CLASS

From Colonial Times
to the Twenty-First Century

PAUL LE BLANC

Illustrations by
MIKE ALEWITZ

Haymarket Books
Chicago, Illinois

First published 1999 by Humanity Books, an imprint of Prometheus Books

This edition published in 2016 by
Haymarket Books
P.O. Box 180165
Chicago, IL 60618
773-583-7884
info@haymarketbooks.org
www.haymarketbooks.org

ISBN: 978-1-60846-625-2

Trade distribution:
In the U.S. through Consortium Book Sales, www.cbsd.com
In the UK, Turnaround Publisher Services, www.turnaround-uk.com
In Canada, Publishers Group Canada, www.pgcbooks.ca
All other countries, Ingram Publisher Services International, ips_intlsales@ingramcontent.com

This book was published with the generous support of the Wallace Action Fund and Lannan Foundation.

Cover design by Rachel Cohen.

Entered into digital printing November 2018.

Library of Congress CIP data is available.

This book is dedicated to

FRANK LOVELL

(1913–1998)

one of many who has taught and inspired me.

Contents

Preface to the 2016 Edition

It is a pleasure to see a new edition of this short history of the U.S. working class made available by Haymarket Books—particularly with a new cover that highlights the diversity of those whose lives and labor have always kept our country running. In the book's introduction, I define what I mean by *working class* (a term I much prefer to the fuzziness of *middle class*)—it is consistent with the recent Occupy movement's notion of "the 99%," which means it refers to most of us, regardless of precise percentages. The richness in composition of today's working-class majority is matched by the richness of our history, which this book seeks to convey.

At the present moment, a majority of the people in the United States seem to face—in some important ways—nastier realities than was the case when I was growing up. What has been made of our country and of our world, by those whose power and policies have been dominant, is shameful and outrageous and horrific. Growing numbers of people are becoming fearful, angry, and restive over this state of affairs, with a sense that things *should* be better than they are. This book helps to show how laboring people in the past faced similar hard times, and through solidarity and struggle they brought about many positive changes in their lives. Some of these changes are still of benefit to us today.

There is much that has happened since the first appearance of this book. Rather than attempting a fifteen-year update, we can put it quite simply: The situation of the broadly defined U.S. working class is worse in 2016 than it was in 1999. Yet there are also new strengths coming to the fore. Surveying the rich diversity of race and ethnicity that makes up our working-class majority, Martin Luther King Jr. commented back in the 1960s: "We may have all come on different ships, but we're in the same boat now." This elemental understanding is shared more widely today than was the case back then, and there has also been, in our society, the deepened awareness that "great social changes are impossible without the feminine ferment" (as Karl Marx once noted). There are still, of course, powerful forces at work to set us against each other, but as the labor radicals of the old Industrial Workers of the World pointed out: "An injury to one is an injury to all." The organized labor movement has "seen better days," to put it mildly. But what doesn't kill us makes us stronger. History shows that hard times, sooner or later, generate hard-fought struggles through which we're capable of winning victories and bringing better times.

It is my belief that we can learn from the past in order to shape a better future. In striving to make this so, we must draw from the inspiring vision, the great underlying spirit, that animated some of labor's greatest spokespeople (some of whose names are unknown), who spoke and wrote and sang about a better world of freedom, truly creative labor, and genuine community that can and must be won for all of us. Elements from such speeches and writings and songs pepper these pages.

In the first edition of this book, I foolishly, absent-mindedly left out a song that has inspired many, and may inspire many more. It grew out of the great Lawrence, Massachusetts, textile strike of 1912, described in these pages. Women played a central role in that hard-fought but successful struggle, and for some this threw into bold relief the passion and strength of the half of humanity whose liberation from oppression is pivotal to the liberation of all. The radical poet James Oppenheim captured that revolutionary spirit in his poem "Bread and Roses." My failure to include it earlier enables me to share it now as the conclusion of this new preface.

> As we come marching, marching in the beauty of the day,
> A million darkened kitchens, a thousand mill lofts gray,
> Are touched with all the radiance that a sudden sun discloses,
> For the people hear us singing: "Bread and roses! Bread and roses!"
>
> As we come marching, marching, we battle too for men,
> For they are women's children, and we mother them again.
> Our lives shall not be sweated from birth until life closes;
> Hearts starve as well as bodies; give us bread, but give us roses!
>
> As we come marching, marching, unnumbered women dead
> Go crying through our singing their ancient cry for bread.

Small art and love and beauty their drudging spirits knew.
Yes, it is bread we fight for—but we fight for roses, too!

As we come marching, marching, we bring the greater days.
The rising of the women means the rising of the race.
No more the drudge and idler—ten that toil where one reposes,
But a sharing of life's glories: Bread and roses! Bread and roses!

Preface

In part, this book has its origins in my origins. Growing up in the small Pennsylvania town of Clearfield, in the 1950s and early 1960s, I learned from my father and mother, Gaston Le Blanc and Shirley Harris Le Blanc, to have a reverence for the labor movement (the organizations of the working class, especially unions), with which they had identified and which they had been part of for many years. My father worked for the United Stone and Allied Products Workers of America, AFL-CIO/CLC (though he had started off in the Unemployed Councils and Workers Alliance of the 1930s); my mother had worked for the United Electrical, Radio and Machine Workers of America (CIO) in the mid-1940s, and after my birth had also done some part-time work for various unions, including the Stoneworkers and the Amalgamated Clothing Workers of America, AFL-CIO. They were mainstays in Clearfield's central labor council. Among my earliest childhood memories are union meetings, picket lines, and Labor Day parades.

The coherence of the past, the meaning of the present, the hope for the future—for all of these things the labor movement was a central reference point. A *union* for them, and for me, meant what the word implies: the coming-together, the shared strength, of the workers. I was taught that the workers joined together to struggle against the rich, powerful, selfish employers who exploited them. Through unions they sought dignity, decent wages and working conditions, a better future. (I think they would have appreciated the pugnacious insight voiced by Martin Glaberman and Seymour Faber: "Unions don't organize workers—workers organize unions.") I was taught labor songs, such as "Solidarity Forever" and "Union Maid," which sometimes the whole family (there were also my sisters, Patty and Nora) would sing to break the tedium of a long car ride,

1

invariably lifting our spirits with a melodic and poetic vision—expressed with spunk and humor and determination—of labor's inspiring cause.

The working class in which I grew up was hardly a romantic abstraction. It consisted of actual people with a great variety of individual characteristics, shapes and sizes and colors, names and faces and ages, strengths and weaknesses, limitations and talents. My generation came of age in a prolonged period of unusual relative prosperity for the U.S. working class. Most of us came from families that were neither rich nor poor, and so we were taught to think of ourselves as "middle class." But the incomes supporting our families came, more often than not, from one or two people who received wages or salaries from an employer who had need of their ability to labor in some blue-collar or white-collar occupation.

Some of the kids I grew up with also came from union families, and we often shared the half-understood notion that unions defended the workers and were "good." But there were many in Clearfield who saw unions as corrupt, greedy, trouble-making institutions. In junior and senior high school I often found myself arguing with certain teachers and fellow students about these matters. It would have been helpful to have a book like this summarizing the history of U.S. labor and offering the actual words of some of its most eloquent spokespeople.

As I got older, I found that much of the U.S. labor movement did not conform to the idealistic vision that had animated my parents. Much of it seemed to find greater success through practices and policies that were less radical, less inclusive, less democratic. In some quarters there was corruption in the narrow sense—racketeering and gangsterism—but the more pervasive corruption involved a "business unionism" that turned away from the expansive vision of labor's cause. Unions were less inclined to embrace the great majority of society's people with the commitment to equal rights and social justice for all. So it seemed to me as a radical activist in the mid-to-late 1960s, and in the 1970s as a union member while employed as a hospital worker, welfare worker, cab driver, shipyard worker, and auto worker.

As it turned out, the "realistic" accommodation to the status quo and the self-satisfied narrowness which characterized so much of the labor movement in the 1950s and 1960s and 1970s contributed to the erosion of its accomplishments and strength in the next two decades. Now more than ever, it is essential for those who would revitalize the labor movement to have a sense of its history and of the goals and ideals that animated its pioneering leaders and activists.

As a history teacher, I have become increasingly aware that one cannot truly understand the development of the United States except as a story largely shaped by those who labor. And while union members have always represented less—often many times less—than 40 percent of the U.S. working class, the struggles of labor's "militant minorities" have sometimes contributed decisively to what has happened in our country. More than once, I have reached for a book such as this—a succinct history with those who spoke for labor in the past having their say—but I have never quite found this specific volume.

In trying to "find" the book I was looking for, I was fortunate to strike up a collaboration with John Hinshaw, a gifted labor historian who wrote an initial draft of this history, which I then revised substantially. As time went on, we found that the book we were collaborating on was going in different directions—at which point we agreed that the two projects (one a little more scholarly, the other a little more popular) each had value, and I moved forward to complete the one, while John moved forward to complete the other. Much of John remains in this volume, just as there is much of me, I'm sure, in the book that he has gone on to produce. At the same time, I see this as very much my own work, and I assume responsibility for any of its deficiencies.

Students and workers whom I've had the opportunity to teach in various classes have, in turn, helped teach me much about history and teaching as I have sought to make available and comprehensible the story of the working class. Decisive in helping to shape this book, such workers and students are also the ones whom I hope will make up the bulk of its readers, since the individual and collective realities of where they came from, who they are, and what they could become have been essential ingredients in why this book came to be.

There are others whose contributions must be acknowledged. For valuable suggestions and kind words of encouragement I would like to thank Elaine Bernard of the Harvard Trade Union Program. Two veteran activists who deserve much thanks for reading through this work and offering good critical feedback are Russ Gibbons, formerly of the United Steelworkers of America, AFL-CIO and for many years editor of *Steel Labor*, more recently of the Philip Murray Labor Institute at the Community College of Allegheny Country, and David Demarest, a professor of English at Carnegie-Mellon University who has for many years been immersed in literature related to the working class of the Pittsburgh area. From the United

Electrical, Radio and Machine Workers of America there is Peter Gilmore, editor of the *UE News*, who provided a very useful critique of an early draft.

Valuable reactions and suggestions on a later version were forthcoming from Michael Yates, who teaches Economics at the University of Pittsburgh-Johnstown and Labor Studies at University of Massachusetts-Amherst. A fine labor historian and friend of many years—Mark McColloch, who heads up the History Department at the University of Pittsburgh's Greensburg campus—reviewed the manuscript in its final stages. Another friend, Dan Kovalik on the legal staff of the United Steelworkers, also shared information and advice, and his enthusiasm and commitment to the cause of labor were a pleasure to behold. Lisa Frank, a fine teacher and colleague in the History Department of Carlow College, also offered encouraging feedback on this project. So did two other friends who have been doing much to deepen our understanding of the North American working class, Paul Buhle at Brown University and Bryan Palmer at Queens University (Canada). The friendship of Carol McAllister—an ethnographer doing exciting work studying family support programs among low-income layers of the working class—has also been invaluable. Frank Lovell, a veteran of the Sailor's Union of the Pacific (AFL) and the United Auto Workers (AFL-CIO), with more than six decades in the labor movement, has been a close friend and a valued teacher, and I dedicate this book to him.

—Paul Le Blanc
April 1998

Postscript (May 21, 1999):

I would like to thank those at Humanity Books who helped with the production of this volume, including Mary A. Read, Tracey Belmont, and Eugene O'Connor. I would like to express my warm thanks to labor muralist Mike Alewitz, whose artistic vision—blending grace and humor—provides an imaginative counterpoint to the text.

Frank Lovell died before this book could be published, but it is a consolation that he was able to read the book in manuscript and knew that I was dedicating it to him. Attending the 1997 AFL-CIO Convention and the 1998 Socialist Scholars Conference with this insightful, admirable working-class militant are among the fond memories that I have of someone who was such a good friend for twenty-five years. He will be missed—but he is part of the still-continuing story reflected in this book.

CARL SANDBURG

The People, Yes (excerpt)

Who knows the people, the migratory harvest hands and berry
    pickers, the loan shark victims, the installment house wolves,
The jugglers in sand and wood who smooth their hands along the
    mold that casts the frame of your motor-car engine,
The metal polishers, solderers, and paint spray hands who put the
    final finish on the car,
The riveters and bolt-catchers, the cowboys of the air in the big
    city, the cowhands of the Great Plains, the ex-convicts, the
    bellhops, redcaps, lavatory men—
The union organizer with his list of those ready to join and those
    hesitating, the secret paid informers who report every move
    toward organizing,
The house-to-house canvassers, the doorbell ringers, the good-
    morning-have-you-heard boys, the strike pickets, the strike-
    breakers, the hired sluggers, the ambulance crew, the ambulance
    chasers, the picture chasers, the meter readers, the oysterboat
    crews, the harborlight tenders—who knows the people?

Who knows this from pit to peak? The people, yes. . . .

"You do what you must—this world and then the next-—one
    world at a time."
The grain gamblers and the price manipulators and the
    stock-market players put their own twist on the text: In the
    sweat of thy brow shalt thou eat thy bread.
The day's work in the factory, mill, mine—the whistle, the bell,
    the alarm clock, the timekeeper and the paycheck, your

number on the assembly line, what the night shift says when the
day shift comes—the blood of years paid out for finished products
proclaimed on billboards yelling at highway travelers in green
valleys—
These are daily program items, values of blood and mind in the every-
day rituals of the people. . . .

This old anvil laughs at many broken hammers.
    There are men who can't be bought.
    There are women beyond purchase.
    The fireborn are at home in fire.
    The stars make no noise.
    You can't hinder the wind from blowing.
    Time is a great teacher.
    Who can live without hope?

In the darkness with a great bundle of grief
    the people march.
In the night, and overhead a shovel of stars for
    keeps, the people march:
                "Where to? what next?"

                                        —Carl Sandburg

Explaining the Title of This Book

A history of the working class in the United States should, first of all, give a sense of what is meant by "the working class in the United States." It means most of us who live in the United States of America—which, unfortunately, has not been the focus of a majority of history books that claim to tell the story of this country. This doesn't make sense, because without the working class there would be no United States. (From a certain point of view, this history book deficiency does make sense, given the biases built into our business-dominated culture.)

The *working class* includes employed people and their family members whose living is dependent on selling labor-power (the ability to work) to employers for wages or salaries; many of these working people are neither rich nor poor but "middle income" (sometimes misleadingly labeled "middle class"), whose living standards have generally stagnated and declined over the past two decades. It also includes the poorly employed and unemployed working-class sectors living below the poverty line, receiving either "starvation wages" or welfare payments. It includes those who—after decades in the labor force—now face an uncertain future in their retirement years. And it includes young people, many of them students, who represent the future of the country and of its working-class majority.

An economic historian named Michel Beaud, surveying the development of various industrial capitalist countries, focused his attention on the proportion of the "active population," or labor force, receiving wages in those countries. He noted, "in the United States in 1880 the figure was 63 percent." Of course, the working class of that time was different in many ways from today's—which encompasses perhaps 80 percent of the population (with many fewer agricultural workers and private servants, but with a greatly expanded white collar and public service sector). We will want to look at how this working class grew, was changed, and also how it changed our country through its own labor and struggles.

The struggles of the U.S. working class have added up to a general struggle for a better life, for more control over one's own situation (which is what the word *freedom* means), and for a general reality characterized by majority rule, or "rule by the people"—which is what *democracy* means. While the United States is often seen as having that type of government, however, democracy in this country has been profoundly affected by the fact that concentrations of economic power have been in the hands of the wealthy few. Unequal economic power naturally translates into unequal political power, and that undermines a genuine "government by the people." The top layer of society, no more than a few percent of the population, consists of those who make their living through the ownership of big business corporations that dominate our economic life. Below this super-rich minority there is a somewhat larger layer of smaller business people, managers, lawyers, doctors, etc., who are also relatively wealthy. It is not these well-to-do layers, however, that hold the hope for the triumph of democracy in the United States.

The needs and aspirations of the top social layers are not necessarily the same as the needs and aspirations of the rest of us. Our "bottom line" is often at odds with that of big companies owned, served, and supported by America's upper classes. Some have argued that the needs of the majority can only be met through rule by the majority. It seems self-evident that the hope for democracy must, almost by definition, be concentrated in the working-class majority rather than in the rich business minority. A consistent democratic outlook assumes that those whose labor and life-activity have been keeping the country running are precisely the people who should run the country.

One might wonder whether "a people" so incredibly diverse as the U.S. working class could ever act on their common interests. It encompasses groups that originally came from all parts of the world: Europe, Africa, the Caribbean, Latin America, Asia. We all don't speak the same languages. Not all of us are "legal." Some of us compete for each other's jobs. Some of us may end up in jail, and others may get jobs as jail-guards. We have different skin colors, genders, and sexual orientations.

We are often deeply divided in religion, ideology, values. Furthermore, although they are the most organized part of the working class, those in unions haven't always built up thoroughly democratic or inclusive or socially conscious institutions. Many non-union workers are indifferent or hostile toward these working-class organizations.

On the other hand, there have always been workers who have struggled to build solidarity in spite of the enormous diversity of the working class. These activists believed that the power of the wealthy minority ultimately derives from keeping the working-class majority divided. Solidarity, they felt, has been our best defense against the power of the privileged, our best hope for making democracy a living reality.

These views—or biases, or values—shape the way this brief history of the U.S. working class has been written. Hopefully it will shed light on the past in a way that can help to illuminate how we might shape the future to bring about a genuine rule by the people, with a better life for all.

Because this is a *short* history, a lot is packed into a very small space—so it is especially important to read as carefully and thoughtfully as possible so that useful information doesn't slip by. Students, union members, and workers who read this book should approach it with critical minds as they utilize it to help make sense of the realities discussed in its pages. To help with this critical thinking process, the book contains a very substantial glossary that provides definitions and discussions of many terms relevant to the history of the U.S. working class. It may be worth browsing through the glossary at your leisure, as well as turning to it whenever you find a word in this text ("working class" or "technology" or "solidarity" or "republic" or "militant" or "indentured servant" or "democracy" or "corporation" or "capitalism") whose meaning you may be at least a little unsure of. Also be aware that there is much that is not in this book, so take advantage of the bibliography to find out where you can get more information and different interpretations, to fill in the gaps and get more details, etc.

Such history as this comes alive most authentically, however, in those who will write its next chapters through what they do in their own lives.

CHAPTER 1
Origins

When Christopher Columbus sailed to the Americas, under the sponsorship of the king and queen of Spain, he assumed that he had arrived in South Asia and that the dark-skinned inhabitants were living on islands east of India. These native American "Indians"—peoples with diverse cultures populating the two American continents—became the victims of invasions from European mercantile empires dominated by competing monarchies in Spain, Portugal, France, Britain, and the Netherlands. Many agricultural, technological, socioeconomic, political, and other achievements of the first inhabitants helped the Europeans to survive their first years in the New World, and some of these were absorbed into the way of life of the early colonial settlers. Much was destroyed, however, as the Europeans sought to subjugate or push aside the "Godless heathens" who had been here first.

In the early 1500s, the Spanish secured domination in the Caribbean, most of South America, and Mexico (including parts of what would later be the United States) for its gold and silver. However, Europeans soon discovered that the real wealth of the Americas lay not so much in its gold as in its fertile land. The land could be turned into private property from which the new owners could squeeze fabulous profits in sugar, "worth its weight in gold" in the growing world market, as well as tobacco, cotton, ranching, etc. Extracting either kind of wealth—from mining or agriculture—required the control of a supply of skilled (if unfree) labor. However, diseases and the brutality of Columbus, Cortez, and others had killed off up to 90 percent of the native population. While the survivors worked in Spanish gold mines, plantations, or ranches, the ruling class sought a new supply of labor, and procuring this labor became yet another lucrative business. Millions of Africans were enslaved and crammed onto slave ships for the "middle passage" to the Americas. It has been estimated that one out of six died on the way. Revolts occurred frequently. Some Africans refused to be enslaved and drowned themselves. Others attacked the crew and occasionally ships were taken over and returned to Africa. Nonetheless, the "West Indies" plantations based on slave labor flourished, and by the 1700s about one-third to one-half of all world commerce depended on the islands of the Caribbean, strategically located between Europe, the American continents, and Africa.

Initially, the Spanish were content to let the colder and goldless regions north of Florida go to whatever empire was desperate enough to seize them. The commercial empires of the Netherlands, France, and Britain competed for dominance in North America. It was the British—colonizing New England and Virginia—who pushed out all rivals: first the Dutch, eventually the French. The British empire's search for a cash crop to rival the Caribbean's lucrative sugar plantations ended when settlers in Virginia discovered tobacco could be sold at enormous profit in Europe. The scramble for the land began in earnest. The work was harsh and the hot climate (combined with overwork) killed most Europeans before they were thirty. But if a settler was cunning enough to obtain good crop land and a regular labor supply, he could grow rich. The colony "built on smoke" boomed. By 1660, 30,000 Europeans and 1,500 Africans or Afro-Caribbeans lived in Virginia.

Seizing the land from its native inhabitants was difficult (early wars in Virginia were bloody and sometimes went badly for the Europeans) but securing a labor supply proved just as tricky. The dominant form of labor was indentured servitude which bound impoverished European laborers to their master for a fixed period of time (between four and seven years) in exchange for a lump sum (often the price of transportation from Europe, a small parcel of forestland, and some household belongings). About two-thirds of all bound servants died before they were freed from service. At first, some African slaves were treated more or less like indentured servants, enjoying minimal legal rights and eventually being freed. Freed bondsmen (and most were men) discovered that the best land had already been taken and thus they were forced to occupy land closer to the frontier with the Indian nations. This pitted oppressed groups against each other—which often happened in American history. The poorer colonists resented that they were restricted from seizing more land from the Indians. They also resented serving as a buffer between the land of the wealthy and Indians' territories.

In 1676, the class and race tensions of colonial Virginia exploded. The trigger came when Nathaniel Bacon, a moderately prosperous planter, organized an illegal attack on Indian settlements in order to seize more land. When he was arrested, his cause attracted the support of landless whites, European servants, and African slaves. Bacon criticized the appointed governor's blatant favoritism toward the rich, especially in the sale of public lands and mistreatment of servants. The poor rallied to Bacon, the governor was driven from the region, and some rich plantations were looted.

By 1677, "Bacon's Rebellion" was crushed. However, the revolt attracted the attention of the English government. Parliament enacted a series of "reforms" that intensified legal distinctions between poor whites and blacks. Landless whites weren't permitted to vote, but they could not be abused as badly as before. African slaves lost whatever rights they had enjoyed. Racial distinctions and divisions were encouraged. Interracial marriage was criminalized, though slave owners were permitted to rape female slaves in order to increase their property. Laws were passed that protected white servants (whose numbers were dropping) while degrading blacks (whose numbers were increasing). White servants could not be whipped naked, but slaves could not only be whipped but mutilated. As historian Edmund Morgan observed, "In order to get work out of men and women who had nothing to gain except the absence of pain, you had to be willing to beat, maim and kill."

Slavery spread throughout the colonies. In eighteenth-century New York City, about 15 percent of the population were slaves. Artisans trained slaves in their crafts and these newly skilled workers thirsted for their freedom as much as any field hand. The system of racism was still evolving and many Irish were treated with the same violence and contempt as Africans. The Irish were not yet considered to be "white" and sometimes made common cause with their African workmates—but joint rebellions of slaves and Irish servants were brutally crushed. Among the enslaved Africans in the countryside, in addition to risk-filled and (as it turned out) doomed efforts at outright rebellion, other forms of resistance became common. Various forms of disobedience, working slowly or poorly, "playing dumb," subtly negotiating better working or living conditions, covert cultural resistance (through music, religion, etc.) were among the many strategies employed by enslaved black laborers.

Slaveowners often relied on beatings, whippings, and torture to maintain their property rights. There was great fear that the slaves would exercise the same brutality to gain their freedom as owners used to maintain their profits. This resulted—whenever slave rebellions seemed possible—in an intensification of brutality to discipline slaves. Frequently slaves would seek freedom by running away from their masters. Many were recaptured and severely punished, but many others were able to reach nonslave areas. Some were able to find refuge with the Indians.

Although slaves existed in the Northern colonies, along with an even larger number of indentured servants (at least half of all immigrants to the colonies—250,000 by 1770), it was free labor that soon became predominant in that region. Here, too, agriculture absorbed the energies of a majority of the colonists in the North (with wheat, corn, fruits, and vegetables taking the place of tobacco and cotton in these colder climates). There were landowners with huge estates, which depended on the hard work of agricultural laborers and tenant farmers. There were also more small family farms than were able to exist in the plantation-dominated South. Some of these were more or less thriving commercial farms run like small businesses, and many were simply subsistence farms on which relatively poor families would eke out a modest but independent existence. There was nothing quite so dramatic as Bacon's Rebellion in the North. Yet growing tensions—sometimes punctuated by violent conflict—naturally developed between wealthy elites and hard-pressed majorities in the rural areas of that region. When news reached the colonies of England's "Glorious Revolution" of 1688 (in which King James II was forced to abdicate in favor of a monarch who would accept the authority of Parliament) this stimulated revolts in New England, New York, Maryland, and the Carolinas that—while not eliminating all popular grievances—established some limits in the authority of the powerful few over the bulk of the colonists.

The absence of a plantation economy in the North contributed to the more rapid development of urbanization. A growing number of Northerners were drawn into port cities such as Boston, Philadelphia, and New York, as well as a growing network of towns. Merchants were the most successful entrepreneurs in such colonies as Massachusetts, New York, and Pennsylvania, and their commerce was dependent on the labor of those engaged in shipbuilding, as well as on the labor of sailors and longshoremen. Other laborers were also needed to sustain the growing urban communities—those engaged in the construction trades, and those engaged in making other things that urban popula- tions might need: weavers and tailors, shoemakers, bakers, carpenters and cabinet makers, blacksmiths and silversmiths, typographical workers and printers, and more. Among those engaged in the skilled trades, the master-craftsman who owned a particular enterprise would be on top, with capable journeymen doing the bulk of the work in the middle, and young apprentices just learning the trade on the bottom. There were also many unskilled day-laborers, servants of various kinds in the homes of the well-to-do, and a variety of small shopkeepers.

The scale of "big cities" in colonial times did not exceed a population of 20,000, and the well-to-do upper classes tended to dominate much of the political and cultural life as they dominated the economy. On the other hand, these thriving commercial centers generated a growing cultural diversity—various religions, various ethnic groups, various occu- pations, various new ideas—which stimulated the inhabitants to think and act in ways that were different from what might be found in more stable or static rural environments. In various churches, taverns, sewing and quilting groups, and town meetings traditions and innovations were critically discussed as people sought to forge a better life for themselves and their children in the New World.

CHAPTER 2

The First American Revolution

Throughout the early 1700s, the commercial empires dominated by the kings of Britain and France engaged in a series of wars over who would control North America. James Fenimore Cooper's romantic classic *Last of the Mohicans*—and the fascinating if gory 1992 motion picture of the same name—give some sense of the last of these conflicts, in which Indians and colonists were used as pawns in European power politics to secure control over profitable raw materials and markets and investment opportunities in the resource-rich New World. After the French were decisively defeated in 1763, the stage was set for the creation of a new nation, created by the mostly European settlers living in Britain's thirteen North American colonies.

Who Made the Revolution and Why

The upper classes in the colonies wanted to be free to make profits without having to put up with restrictive economic policies imposed by the king and the upper classes of Britain. But this wasn't enough of a social base to win a revolution. The bulk of the colonists were working people—laboring on small farms, laboring as skilled artisans and craftsmen, laboring in small family-owned shops, laboring as unskilled urban workers and servants, etc.—who wanted a better life, more opportunities to develop themselves, more dignity and freedom from hereditary and arrogant elites. Some of them increasingly desired a political reality that would be more under "the rule of the people"—which the rich elites fearfully referred to as "mob-ocracy," but which today is known as *democracy*.

One of the key incidents leading up to the Revolution was the Boston Massacre. Although racism had been growing in the Americas, it was an interracial crowd that confronted and was fired upon by British soldiers

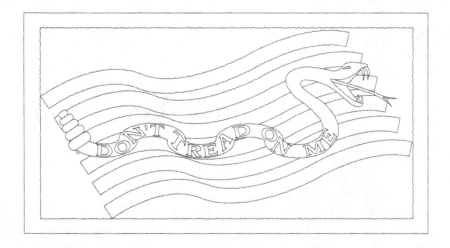

in 1770. Boston's artisans, craftsmen, and laboring poor—many of whom were drawn to the Sons of Liberty by radical organizer Samuel Adams— were acquainted with the pamphlets that criticized the taxes and special privileges of the imperial regime. But what triggered their anger was that British soldiers stationed in their city competed for jobs in rope shops or "ropewalks." Soldiers fired into the rowdy demonstration and British troops shot and killed five Bostonians. All were workers. Crispus Attucks was a half-black, half-Indian sailor. Patrick Carr was an Irish-born leather worker. The others were native-born rope workers, sailors, or journeymen.

The actions of urban "mobs" proved as important to the early revolutionary cause as the eloquence of Thomas Jefferson, Benjamin Franklin, or others. Urban workers literally attacked the agents of the English crown and destroyed property, as in the Boston Tea Party in 1774. Throughout the Revolutionary War that raged from 1775 to 1783, farmers, laborers, and artisans made up the bulk of the revolutionary army and guerrilla bands that ultimately defeated the British army.

The leaders of the American Revolutionaries were wealthy Northern merchants such as John Hancock, well-to-do lawyers such as John Adams, rich slaveowners such as Thomas Jefferson and George Washington, prosperous self-made businessmen such as printer-publisher Benjamin Franklin. They opposed rule by kings and favored the independence of the colonies, although most of the "founding fathers" were also inclined to believe that people of "quality"—that is, people such as themselves— should run society in the public interest. But it was the democratic ideology expressed by the revolutionary firebrand Thomas Paine that proved capable of inspiring masses of people. Protesting against "monarchical tyranny" and "aristocratical tyranny," and insisting that "exalting one man so greatly above the rest cannot be justified on the equal rights of nature," Paine denounced King George III as "a royal brute" and insisted that it was "Common Sense" that there should be an independent government based on "a large and equal representation" of the people. Such notions were incorporated by Jefferson into the Declaration of Independence of 1776:

> We hold these truths to be self-evident, that all men are created equal, that they are endowed by their Creator with certain inalienable rights, that among these are life, liberty and the pursuit of happiness. That to secure these rights, governments are instituted among men, deriving their just powers from the consent of the governed. That whenever any form of government becomes destructive of these ends, it is the right of the people to alter or to abolish it, and to institute new government, laying its foundation on such principles and organizing its powers in such form, as to them shall seem most likely to effect their safety and happiness.

Thousands of farmers and field hands, small shopkeepers, artisans and craftsmen, skilled and unskilled laborers rallied to this cause, capturing two British armies and defeating what was then the most powerful nation on Earth before it was all over in 1783. The war for independence—and the ideals that inspired it—had a profound impact throughout the world. The American Revolution went beyond a struggle for "home rule" (independence) to become a struggle over "who would rule at home."

In 1786, for example, impoverished and debt-ridden Massachusetts farmers—mostly Revolutionary War veterans following Daniel Shays—rose up against the state government that took the side of the rich against them. As General Henry Knox wrote to his well-to-do friend George Washington, "[T]heir creed is that the property of the United States has been protected from the confiscation of Britain by the joint exertions of all, and therefore should be the common property of all." Knox spoke for many of his class when he concluded that "our Government must be braced, changed, or altered to secure our lives and property." People who worked with their hands had their own sense of what the new country should be and fought against the elitism that was the norm among our "founding fathers," most of whom favored a *republic* (government by elected representatives) in which only "qualified" people—white male property-owners—should have the right to vote.

Economy and Government

Many questions faced the new American Republic. Would the poor, laborers without property, women, or immigrants be able to participate in its political life? To the extent that the Republic would be democratic, should the ideal of equal rights be limited to elections and economic opportunity, or should it permeate all aspects of life? And some—such as Tom Paine—raised the explosive question of whether human slavery was compatible with the revolutionary ideals expressed in the Declaration of Independence. Viewing "the most horrid of all traffics, that of human flesh," as being on the same plane as "murder, robbery, lewdness, and barbarity," Paine had insisted as early as 1775 on the need for "continental legislation which shall put a stop to the importation of Negroes for sale, soften the hard fate of those already here, and in time procure their freedom."

Even radical ideologists of this time were influenced by views expressed by the Scottish philosopher-economist Adam Smith, whose classic book *The Wealth of Nations* (1776) described the increasingly dominant capitalist economy. According to Smith, society would benefit from economic liberty: a market economy (that is, a buying and selling economy), in which the private ownership and control of the economy was exercised by a minority of profit-minded businessmen, would create general prosperity. Smith was an advocate of *laissez-faire* (French for "leave alone") economic policies—the notion that the government should not interfere in the economy, letting businessmen do whatever they wish to make profits, which would presumably result in a full-bodied economic development that would generate prosperity. To revolutionaries like Tom Paine, this seemed an advance over the mercantilist efforts of the British government to regulate American economic life in the interests of the Crown. But liberty in economic realms led to concentrations of wealth and power which threatened the democracy that people like Paine also fiercely supported. (In later years Paine reflected that "the accumulation of personal property is, in many instances, the effect of paying too little for the labor that produced it; the consequence of which is, that the working hand perishes in old age, and that the employer abounds in affluence." In the opinion of the old revolutionary, "the contrast of affluence and wretchedness is like dead and living bodies chained together.") This contradiction animated struggles of workers, farmers, and other "producers." These struggles over who would rule, and in whose interests society would be ruled, was one of the factors that has fundamentally shaped U.S. history.

Such tensions can be seen in the struggle around the U.S. Constitution in 1787–1789. Despite their sacrifices, there were no poor farmers, laborers, or artisans among the "founding fathers" who wrote the new Constitution. Wealthy men had a peculiar view of liberty. Many of the Constitution's key features (allowing the imposition of property limits on voting, indirect election of the Senate, the electoral college, appointment of judges) were designed precisely to limit popular pressure on government. Furthermore, while the Constitution has numerous provisions designed to protect private property, it initially had little or nothing to say about human rights. Popular agitation helped to add ten amendments (the "Bill of Rights") to the Constitution, protecting citizens' rights to freedom of speech, assembly, religion, etc.*

Property rights were central to how freedom was defined in the United States. The role of government was to expand the marketplace in order to expand Americans' opportunities to practice their liberty. The westward expansion of the United States, wiping out Indians and stealing their land, to make way for "a white man's republic," was carried out under the banner of bringing an untamed wilderness under the control of a new nation that would offer liberty and prosperity for all hardworking citizens. This dual character of the United States—defense of a republic of the "common man" in the face of the power of the British empire, but also a lust for expanding the country's boundaries—was reflected in the War of 1812. The U.S. government also encouraged industrialization to enhance this liberty and prosperity, and to break the country's old colonial dependence on Europe.

---

* The Bill of Rights protects the rights of citizens from incursions by the federal government. The Fourteenth Amendment, at the conclusion of the Civil War, extended these rights by protecting them from incursions by state and local governments. But there was little thought of the need to protect the rights of citizens from incursions by private interests—such as individuals or businesses having great concentrations of economic power.

Reform Struggles

Most workers were proud of their role in helping to found the Republic, but economic development was changing how work was done, sometimes in ways that hurt them. The spread of the capitalist marketplace helped to break down the craft or artisan system which had regulated manufacturing workers since the Middle Ages. Instead of progressing from apprentices to journeymen and then to self-employed master-craftsmen, many apprentices evolved into permanent wage laborers. The craft system assumed that everyone would eventually become a master, but an indication that things had changed was the development of unions open only to journeymen who sometimes conducted strikes against the masters. One of the first strikes occurred in 1768, when twenty journeymen tailors in New York City struck against a reduction in wages. Workers were initially hesitant to exclude employers from their organizations. As late as 1817, a journeymen printers' association only reluctantly excluded master printers from membership. But with the advancing development of the capitalist economy workers came to see a fundamental division between themselves and the enterprising businessmen for whom they worked. The notion of the modern *trade union*—workers in a particular workplace or occupation joining together to compel their employers to give them higher wages, better working conditions, a shorter workday, dignity on the job, etc.—was seen as extremely radical not only by businessmen but also by many workers.

Many more working people focused their attentions on the political arena. Raising such slogans, reminiscent of the American Revolution, as "No Taxation Without Representation" and "Liberty or Revolution," farmers and journeymen attacked property restrictions on voting throughout the first decades of the Republic. In the Northern states, where the working class was largest, slavery was gradually abolished. By the 1830s, many Northern states had granted voting rights to all free, white males. Upper-class resistance to extending the right to vote was overcome only through mass pressure—and sometimes through the threat of worse.

And yet, as we have seen before, there was also a tendency for oppressed groups to compete with each other. Sometimes, as in Pennsylvania, the reform extending the right to vote for white working-class males had the effect of limiting the voting rights of black workers, and many working-class activists believed women (also denied voting rights) shouldn't be economically independent—and so they worked to limit the jobs women could hold. Many poor immigrants were also viewed as lacking "republican virtue" as their poverty could make them pawns of the wealthy. Immigrants, the bulk of whom came from Ireland and Germany (until the 1880s), were often targets of attacks by anti-immigrant gangs. Many workers supported the ongoing genocide against the Indian nations, and the brutal war (1846–1848) against the new Republic of Mexico. For many, democratic rights in the U.S. Republic should be limited to Protestant white males, and the bold citizens of the United States should dominate the North American continent by sweeping aside the "colored" peoples standing in their way.

At the same time, the ideals of the American Revolution continued to inspire many people—including some among the growing working class—to push for political and social reforms that would make the radical-democratic promises of the Declaration of Independence, especially the notion of equal rights for all, a reality. This reforming fervor resulted in struggles for public schools to benefit all children, the spread of volunteer associations (such as fire brigades) to benefit working-class communities, the more just and humane treatment of those living in poverty, campaigns against alcohol abuse, the spread of the abolitionist movement against slavery, and the struggle for women's rights. Some reformers went so far as to set up experimental utopian socialist communities in which people could live and work together according to the Golden Rule ("do unto others as you would have them do unto you"), all sharing equally in the work and in the fruits of their labor.

The democratic notions of equal rights and rule by the people did not always harmonize with the dynamics of U.S. economic development. Trying to reconcile revolutionary ideals with the realities of a changing society was complicated. Making this task more difficult were the profound changes that resulted from the Industrial Revolution.

CHAPTER 3

Industrial Revolution

The Industrial Revolution began in Britain in the late 1700s. It involved the replacement of muscle power with machine power, made more possible thanks to the development of the steam engine. In later years, other forms of energy (electricity, the internal-combustion engine, nuclear power, etc.) came into play. The constantly improving technology (tools) of the Industrial Revolution resulted in dramatically rising productivity: more products being created with less labor. This created the possibility of fabulous increases in the profits of businessmen, the possibility of rising living standards for working people, and ongoing conflicts over which possibilities would be realized.

Machines and Labor

The spread of the Industrial Revolution to the United States in the early 1800s dramatically changed workers, workplaces, and the United States as a whole. In the "high-tech" industries of the early 1800s, water- or steam-powered machines were used to increase production. Textile mills relied on waterfalls to power their machine looms. By the 1830s, steam engines were used on ships, railroads, and in a growing number of factories. However, the replacement of steam for hand power was just one aspect of the changes wrought by industrialization.

Originally, the new textile mills in Lowell, Massachusetts were seen as providing an ideal opportunity for New England farm girls to earn extra money for their families while at the same time bettering themselves through benevolently supervised workplaces and communities set up by the employers. Within a few years, however, the drive for increased profits caused the factory-owners to drive their young workers harder and harder—and then turn to the labor of poor immigrants whom they

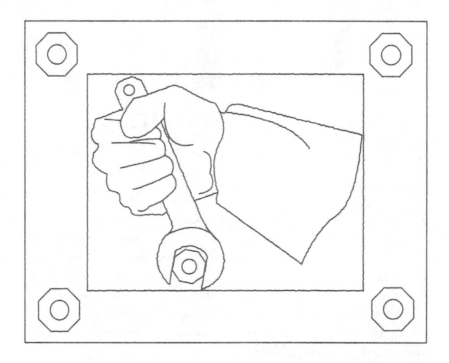

hoped to be able to boss around more easily. Workplaces grew larger, and textile factories employed hundreds of children, young women, and men. Wages were low, hours long, conditions increasingly poor. Many New England factories especially relied on indigent women and children who were forced to work at jobs no one else would take.

It is not the case that factories grew bigger because of any technical needs inherent in industrialization. Employers were simply looking for more effective ways to control their labor force, which enabled them to maximize their profits by squeezing more work out of their employees. When an employer pays wages to a worker, he is simply buying that worker's *ability to work*: the trick then is to squeeze out from the wage-worker as much *actual work* as possible. Even small employers found that by dividing the work process, which gave them more control over the labor of their workers, they could maximize production and profits.

In 1776, for example, shoemakers were generally self-employed artisans who produced entire shoes at their own, often leisurely, pace. By the 1840s, skilled shoemakers had given way to shoe workers, each of whom made just one part of the shoe for their employer, often laboring twelve to sixteen hours a day. The product of their labor was then sold to Northern city dwellers, farmers, or to Southern planters who bought cheap shoes for their slaves. In 1850, the Lynn, Massachusetts, Board of Health found that overwork and poverty meant that shoemakers had a life expectancy twenty years lower than farmers. Nonetheless, industry attracted many new migrants to cities, which grew at an enormous rate and increasingly became the site of the rising factory system.

Because of the high cost of land in New York City, no large factories developed there. Instead, tens of thousands of men, women, and children produced ready-to-wear clothing in small sweatshops or in their own homes. New York's large immigrant population created a vast reserve army of the unemployed and wages remained painfully low. Tailors bitterly explained that a man needed the employment of his wife and several children to survive in the trade. Thousands of single women were tailors, and they often lived on the edge of starvation. After a few years of intense work, seamstresses could be identified on the street by the stooped shoulders and deteriorated vision that inevitably crippled them.

Factories influenced other parts of the economy. As relatively cheap factory-made shoes and textiles became widely available, fewer and fewer families made their own shoes or spun their own fabric. Farmers no longer ground their grain at home but took it to a local flour mill. The drive to produce goods for the market drove not only industrialists but farmers. The growth of industrializing European cities created a growing outlet for Southern cotton as well as Northern grain. Large amounts of flour would be ground in mechanized mills, shipped across upstate New York on the Erie Canal (much of it dug by Irish immigrants), and then shipped to Europe. As people began to purchase more manufactured goods, the relative importance of the cash economy grew. Even small-scale farmers produced more cash crops during the growing season and increasingly worked for wages in the winters.

The Rise of Labor Organizations

The experience of working for wages for an entire lifetime was still relatively rare. Prior to the 1820s, even most tailors, shoemakers, or other artisans expected to work for others until they learned the trade and went into business for themselves. Most early factory workers in Lowell's textile mills (especially the large number of young women) only worked a few years, saving money to begin their own homes. Being permanently tied to an employer for your livelihood seemed incompatible with republican virtues of self-reliance and independence. Skilled factory workers, well-off artisans, or craft workers such as carpenters often looked down on poor workers or factory hands, especially women and recent immigrants from Ireland or Germany. Workers especially feared becoming "wage slaves," an indication of the growing interpenetration of the free and slave labor systems.

Although it promoted industry as well as slavery, the government was hostile to trade unionists. Unions were frequently labeled "conspiracies" and banned by law. In 1836, a New York judge fined twenty union tailors, lecturing them that unions were an "unlawful combination" that limited the "liberty" of employers. These "un-American" unions were "mainly upheld by foreigners," in the good judge's opinion. The city's unions rallied over 25,000 New Yorkers, 10 percent of the city, to protest this trial. Up in Boston, the young carpenter and labor agitator Seth Luther, in tones reminiscent of old Tom Paine, scoffed that "the Declaration of Independence was the work of a combination, and was as hateful to the traitors and tories of those days as combinations among workingmen are now to the avaricious monopolist and purse proud aristocrat." Many male unionists did not extend this level of solidarity toward women workers. In 1819, New York's tailor's union threatened to go on strike against the increasing number of women tailors in their trade, arguing that their presence was helping to depress wage rates. On the other hand, Seth Luther argued that "unless we have the female sex on our side, we cannot hope to accomplish the object we have in view."

As industrialization advanced, so did efforts of the growing class of wageworkers to protect their rights and dignity. "As our fathers resisted unto blood the lordly avarice of the British ministry," proclaimed the striking factory girls of the Lowell textile mills, "so we, their daughters, never will wear the yoke that has been prepared for us." Similar sentiments motivated union organizing among an increasing number of occupations: carpenters, typographical workers, masons, shoeworkers, textile workers, cigarmakers, and others. Some sought to create independent workers' parties, many were absorbed (and ultimately frustrated) by the Democratic Party that was reorganized under the rags-to-riches slaveowner Andrew Jackson. Labor reform struggles for such things as the ten-hour workday also attracted much working-class support. "Our cause is the cause of truth—of justice and humanity," Seth Luther proclaimed, adding: "Let us be determined no longer to be deceived by the cry of those who produce nothing and who enjoy all, and who insult-ingly term us—the farmers, the mechanics, and the laborers—the lower orders—and exultingly claim our homage for themselves as the *higher* orders—while the Declaration of Independence asserts that 'All men are created equal.'"

Hard Times

But fluctuating and volatile economic realities made it difficult to sus-tain labor organizations. The Industrial Revolution resulted in a vast increase in the production of most goods which often outstripped effec-tive demand; the result was severe depressions or "gluts." Employers' drive for efficient production threw large numbers of employees out of work but politicians believed that if the government intervened to help unemployed workers it would destroy their sense of self-sufficiency. Thus private charity and public relief were both meager and punitive. Workingmen's Parties and unions often argued that governments should provide public works, and at the local level, their demands were some-times met. However, publicly run unemployment insurance or schools (to educate the poor and take children out of the labor market) or other "safety net" programs would not be implemented until decades later. As a result, when hard times came, as they inevitably did, the old, the very young, the crippled, and unlucky suffered. Families often lost what few possessions they had and sometimes starved.

Of all sectors of the U.S. labor force, blacks had the hardest time of all. While slavery had been abolished in the North by the early 1800s, most white Americans continued to ostracize and oppress African Americans. Blacks were denied employment in most industries. Generally forced out of skilled trades by competing white workers, a majority of black work-ers could only find lower-paid unskilled labor, and this too was often denied them as unskilled immigrants from Ireland and other impover-ished European regions flooded the job market. It was deeply ingrained in the dominant culture—and struck deep roots in the consciousness of most native-born and immigrant white workers—that blacks were infe-rior beings. White workers generally believed that it would be degrading to work beside such inferiors or to see them receive equal wages, and most employers were very much of the same mind. For many free blacks only the most menial jobs—"drive a carriage, carry a straw basket after the boss, and brush his boots, or saw wood and run errands," as one free black put it—were available, and some families were able to survive only through the labor of black women working as laundresses.

While free blacks were poorer than white workers, blacks' meager earnings supported a wide range of abolitionist newspapers. African Americans often had firsthand experience with the brutalities of slavery and consequently their brand of abolitionism was far more militant than that of well-heeled white moralists. In the early 1800s, many white abolitionists still wanted to resolve the blight of slavery from U.S. soil by resettling blacks in Africa or in black-ruled Haiti (after that Caribbean island country's momentous antislavery revolution and liberation wars of 1791–1803). Only free blacks and white radicals in the U.S. abolitionist movement wanted simply to abolish slavery and secure equal rights for all irrespective of color.

In general, all nonwhite workers faced persecution in the growing Republic. California and Texas had been part of Mexico but were taken over by the United States through the Mexican War of the 1840s. The majority population of the Mexican Americans, who were there first, were generally barred from voting and were forced into the lowest level of the economy. By the 1840s, California attracted not only numerous white settlers, but also Chinese who came to the "golden mountain" to work as miners and railroad workers. Chinese immigrants received an especially vicious reception by white workers. Their thrift and efficiency angered white workers who accused them of being tools of monopolists who conspired to lower the price of labor. Anti-Chinese laws succeeded in restricting immigrants to a handful of menial jobs such as laundry worker, laborer, and street peddler. One historian referred to the Chinese as the "indispensable enemy" of the labor movement in California, because opposition to "coolie labor" was a central rallying cry of white workers.

CHAPTER 4

Slave Labor, Free Labor

The upper class of Northern businessmen was profoundly transformed by industrialization, as manufacturers became increasingly more important than the once-predominant merchants in the region's economy. Southern slaveowners were also directly affected by the Industrial Revolution. The development of the cotton gin made it easier, and more profitable, to separate seeds from fibers, and the rapid growth of textile manufacturing in Great Britain (and later in New England) made Southern cotton more lucrative. The doubts about the virtue of slavery, which some liberal-minded slaveowners like Thomas Jefferson had entertained amid the radicalism of the American Revolution, quickly gave way to the militant defense and aggressive expansion of slavery among the powerful Southern planters. The slaveowners sought to expand not only the number of slaves they owned but also their land holdings, often by moving westward. Tobacco and cotton production wore out the land faster than other kinds of farming, and for this reason too the slave system needed to expand.

The Industrial Revolution had a different impact in the North, where manufacturing rather than agriculture became increasingly predominant. Northern industrialists relied on high tariffs that would be imposed by the government to keep out cheaper and often better-made goods from England. They also wanted more government dollars spent on internal improvements (transportation systems, urban improvements, education, etc.) to create the infrastructure so important to industrialization. (Thus the "self-reliant" businessman of laissez-faire capitalism was a myth, even at the dawn of the industrial age.) The Northern economy was dependent on a system of free labor, not slave labor, and this also had important consequences for the region's political development. For example, the bulk of the voters—small farmers and workers—favored policies that

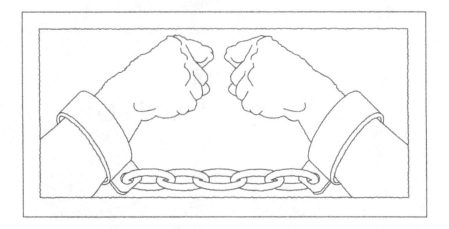

would advance economic opportunities for them, especially the banning of slavery throughout the North and in the Western territories.

Intensifying political tensions between North and South resulted. Slaveowners wanted to retain their control of the federal government. This would enable them to prevent high tariffs and what they viewed as "excessive" expenditures on internal improvements (which were not beneficial to their own economic needs) and to prevent restrictions on slavery. Many in the North, on the other hand, feared that their own freedoms and economic needs were being undermined by what they viewed as an antidemocratic "Slave Power." This fear rose as Southern political leaders systematically sought to add new slave territories to the United States in order to retain their influence over the federal government. Although slaves were not citizens, they were counted as three-fifths of a voter for the purpose of allocating seats in the House of Representatives, yet the more populous North still had a majority. If there were more free states than slave states, the balance in the Senate as well as in the House would tilt against the South—endangering what the plantation elite viewed as a superior way of life.

In the 1830s, the economic and political calculus of slavery propelled whites, often illegally, across the U.S. border into Texas and California, which were then part of the Republic of Mexico. Eventually, these English-speaking "Mexicans" fought "wars of independence." In 1846–1848, a U.S. war of conquest resulted in Mexico losing two-thirds of its land. Mexican landowners were swindled of their property and poorer Mexicans became new sources of cheap labor for plantations, railroads, and industry. While California became a free-labor state, slaveowners hoped that new slave states could be added to the South by additional wars. Cuba and Central America were considered the most desirable prospects. In fact, throughout the 1850s, a Southerner named William Walker attempted several "revolutions" in Central America. While he was a hero in New Orleans, and was rescued several times by U.S. warships, he was eventually captured and executed in Central America.

Moderate politicians of the North and South continually searched for compromises. Until 1850, states were admitted to the Union in order to preserve the balance between free and slave states. The admission of California in 1850 tilted the balance against slave states, but Southern politicians, who were often slaveowners, succeeded in preventing Congress from discussing the petitions of Northern abolitionists, signed by hundreds of thousands of workers, farmers, and members of the middle classes. Slaveowners convinced Congress to tighten laws against runaway slaves, and also to allow the spread of slavery to any newly admitted states if this was the will of the (white male) majority of settlers in those areas. This created an explosive situation—including a virtual civil war in the Kansas territory in the late 1850s.

Many enslaved African Americans also had strong opinions on the question of slavery. They had come to the conclusion—as the ex-slave Frederick Douglass put it—that "slaveowners who would have gladly made me believe that they were merely acting under the authority of God, in making a slave of me, and in making slaves of others," were in fact "robbers and deceivers." Even "good masters" who treated slaves well caused "dreams of freedom [to] intrude" into the consciousness of the slave: "Give him a bad master, and he aspires to a good master; give him a good master, and he wishes to become his own master. Such is human nature." Douglass—observing efforts to pit blacks and whites against each other—insightfully noted common qualities of slave labor and wage labor:

> The slaveholders, with a craftiness peculiar to themselves, by encouraging the enmity of the poor, laboring white man against the blacks, succeeds in making the said white man almost as much a slave as the black slave himself. The differences between the white slave and the black slave is this: the latter belongs to *one* slaveholder, and the former belongs to *all* slaveholders collectively. The white slave has taken from him by indirection what the black slave has taken from him directly, and without ceremony. Both are plundered, and by the same plunderers. The slave is robbed by his master of all his earnings, above what is required for his bare physical

necessities; and the white man is robbed by the slave system, of the just results of his labor, because he is flung into competition with a class of laborers who work without wages.

The fact remained that while most white workers hated slavery, many also hated slaves and free blacks. Whites feared becoming "wage slaves," but in a country founded on slaughtering Indians and enslaving blacks, many workers fell victim to racism. For instance, when Frederick Douglass's owner hired him out to a Baltimore shipyard, he was beaten up by two Irish immigrants. However, another Irish worker helped Douglass to escape to freedom. Racism was infectious, but there were healthy countertendencies. Some immigrant workers in the 1840s and 1850s opposed slavery from deep and expansive democratic convictions, strongly supporting the abolitionist cause. Many Germans were forced to flee to the United States after the failure of democratic revolutions at home; these immigrants—which included workers attracted to radical "equal rights" and socialist ideas—were inclined to view the eradication of slavery as a victory for workers everywhere. Harriet Beecher Stowe's antislavery novel *Uncle Tom's Cabin*, which powerfully emphasized the humanity of the slaves, won many more working people to the abolitionist cause.

Regardless of the variety of their specific outlooks, a growing majority of Northern working people rallied to the cause of challenging the expansion of "the Slave Power." Many responded with enthusiasm to the 1860 presidential candidate who said to striking shoe workers: "I am glad to see that a system of labor prevails in New England under which laborers can strike when they want to, where they are not obliged to labor whether you pay them or not. I like the system that lets a man quit when he wants to, and wish it might prevail everywhere. One of the reasons I am opposed to slavery is right here." This was Abraham Lincoln, whose support of "free labor" as against slavery caused him to insist "that labor is prior to, and independent of capital; that, in fact, capital is the fruit of labor, and could never have existed if labor had not first existed; that labor can exist without capital, but that capital could never have existed without labor. Hence . . . labor is the superior . . . greatly superior to capital." Lincoln was committed to an economic program in which labor and capital would cooperate in dramatically furthering the industrial development of the United States. That would presumably lead to expanding jobs, profits, prosperity, and democracy. Championed by the new Republican Party, this program was challenged by the Democratic Party in which the slaveowners were a dominant force.

CHAPTER 5

The Second American Revolution

By the 1850s, the newly formed Republican Party had emerged as the representative of "free soil, free labor and free men." The party stood for the hopes of abolitionists who opposed slavery and many Northern farmers, laborers, and industrialists who hoped simply to contain slavery. A key goal was to eliminate the threat of slaveowners' control over the government which was limiting the growth of the Northern economy (and thus Northerners' liberty). But the Republicans would eventually be forced to wage total war on slavery.

Antislavery Struggle

While white abolitionists or Abraham Lincoln are often credited with freeing the slaves, many overlook the crucial role played by free black workers and slaves themselves. Southern planters had long boasted that "their" slaves were ignorant "Sambos," too simpleminded to survive without them. They countered abolitionist tracts by saying that slaves were content, but the planter aristocracy lived in constant fear of slave rebellions. Their fears were well-founded. In 1831, a model slave, Nat Turner, led a rebellion that killed sixty whites. When John Brown and two dozen others raided the federal armory at Harpers Ferry, Virginia in 1859, their plan was to provide rebel slaves with the weapons to free themselves. Most of Brown's men were killed by federal troops, and he was hanged after a sensational trial, but his martyrdom inspired many abolitionists.

One of John Brown's supporters was the African American abolitionist leader Frederick Douglass. Holding back from Brown's desperate

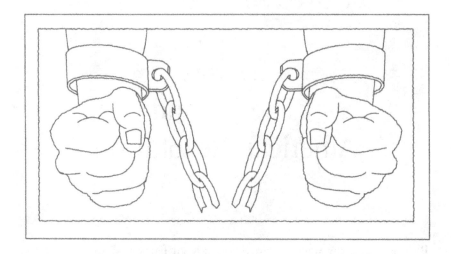

effort because he questioned its practicality, he nonetheless embraced its underlying motivations. In 1857, Douglass had eloquently given voice to essential elements of what would later come to be known as "political science" as well as a fundamental principle of the labor movement:

> The whole history of progress of human liberty shows that all concessions made to her august claims have been born of earnest struggle.... If there is no struggle, there is no progress. Those who profess to favor freedom and yet deprecate agitation are men who want crops without plowing up the ground, they want rain without thunder and lightning. They want the ocean without the awful roar of its many waters.
>
> This struggle may be a moral one, or it may be a physical one, and it may be both moral and physical, but it must be a struggle. Power concedes nothing without a demand. It never did and it never will. Find out just what any people will quietly submit to and you have found out the exact measure of injustice and wrong which will be imposed upon them, and these will continue till they are resisted with either words or blows, or with both. The limits of tyrants are prescribed by the endurance of those whom they oppress.... Men may not get all they pay for, but they must certainly pay for all they get. If we ever get free from the oppressions and wrongs heaped upon us, we must pay for their removal. We must do this by labor, by suffering, by sacrifice, and if needs be, by our lives and the lives of others.

The song "John Brown's Body" became a favorite of abolitionists and was popular among some Northern troops in the early days of the Civil

War. (Significantly, the song was adapted at the beginning of the Civil War to become the "Battle Hymn of the Republic," with words by Julia Ward Howe that essentially repeat the insights expressed by Frederick Douglass. It later was transformed yet again into the labor anthem "Solidarity Forever"—see page 69). An increasing number of Northern working people were rallying to the cause of—as Lincoln later put it—"a nation conceived in liberty" which, "with its institutions, belongs to the people who inhabit it" and should be subject to a government whose policies would be determined by the majority.

War

The threat to the system of slavery posed by the presidential election of Abraham Lincoln caused the majority of Southern states dominated by the slaveowners to break away from the United States. While some poor white farmers and workers in the South were hostile to the new Confederate States of America controlled by the rich plantation owners, many rallied to the defense of their states and local communities, and to a way of life in which—no matter how poor—whites were seen as superior to blacks. This "War for Southern Independence" waged from 1861 to 1865 was the most destructive in U.S. history. The Confederate cause was undermined from the very beginning because the North was able to mobilize a much larger population of working people, and a much more advanced industrial economy. And in the very heart of the Confederacy there was something that doomed its cause from the beginning: millions of African Americans who did not accept the slave-labor system that kept them in bondage.

Slaves could be whipped, but planters could not force them to work efficiently (although they were efficient enough when working on their own garden plots). In fact, during the Civil War, slaves' notorious "inefficiency" mushroomed into what W. E. B. Du Bois termed a *general strike* that crippled the Southern economy. As soon as the Northern army began to occupy parts of the South, large numbers of slaves began to escape to its lines. Initially, the Northern army returned slaves to their owners and refused to let Northern blacks join the army.

At the early stages of the war, trade unionists and immigrant societies joined the Northern army en masse. But as the massive battles of the war consumed so many lives, the U.S. government was compelled to begin drafting soldiers rather than simply relying on volunteers. The draft proved extremely unpopular, especially as the rich could pay for someone else to serve in their place. By 1863, poor Irish rioted against the war and blacks, leaving dozens of black workers dead. Desperate for troops, Lincoln agreed to let blacks join the army, and black troops often fought with incredible ferocity. The North increasingly fought a war against the Southern economy, finding it necessary to liberate slaves in the process. "The War Between the States" had been turned into a war of liberation. (A sense of the war's nature is captured in such films as *Gettysburg* and *Glory*.)

Some later historians termed it the "Second American Revolution" because it destroyed the institution of slavery and advanced the most radical conceptions of 1776. As Lincoln put it in his 1863 Gettysburg Address, many thousands were giving their lives to preserve a republic "dedicated to the proposition that all men are created equal" and overtly committed to "government of the people, by the people and for the people."

Reconstruction

A key to victory was the Emancipation Proclamation, explicitly making the abolition of slavery a centerpiece of the struggle, but when the North finally won the Civil War a question remained: the African American labor force was now free, but free to do what? The Republican Party wanted to stay in power in order to pursue those economic industrialization policies thwarted by the Southern plantation-owners before the Civil War. To achieve this, the Republicans needed a voting base in the South, and they consequently gave black men the right to vote. (Most planters or Confederate politicians—the old Southern ruling elite—were not allowed to vote or serve in government.) Freedmen considered voting desirable, but secondary to desires to reunite families, gain access to the land, and acquire an education. Southern black and white Republicans allocated funds to expand the infrastructure necessary for industry (roads, railroads, harbors). Many humane reforms were adopted that were beneficial to the lower classes. Perhaps most importantly, public schools were built for poor whites and blacks for the first time.

But the most radical of the Republicans insisted that the lower-class majority would not be able to preserve its political power unless it could also secure economic power. They proposed that the big plantations of the old Southern elite be confiscated by the government, and the land be equally divided ("forty acres and a mule," according to one popular slogan) among ex-slaves and loyal poor whites. This proved to be too radical a demand for most political and economic leaders in the North, who feared that such a violation of rich people's "property rights" in the South would give working people in the North similar ideas about what should be done with industrial property. The Southern plantation owners got to keep their land, and this concentration of economic power was eventually translated into the reconquest of political power.

The fragile political alliance of poor whites and freedmen collapsed as the federal government allowed the old planter class to launch a wave of terror. Terrorist and paramilitary groups such as the Ku Klux Klan began by killing outspoken blacks, but also white "race traitors," then increasingly prevented or intimidated most Southern Republicans from voting. By 1877 Northern political and business leaders were prepared to accept the return to power of the old Southern elite, which rallied the bulk of white workers and small farmers in the region under the banner of white supremacy. This acceptance by Northern leaders was based on a gentlemen's agreement that the Southern leaders would accept national economic policies facilitating the continued development of industrial capitalism. The South's "new Democrats" went on to pass "Jim Crow" laws that eliminated black political rights and imposed racial segregation. They also limited black rights to change jobs, rolled back publicly financed education, and expanded the use of convict labor. All of these policies kept Southern laborers—white and black—poor, uneducated, and at the mercy of the employing class.

Survival of the Fittest?

The war had transformed the economy of the United States. Sweeping laws were passed that protected industries, created a national network of railroads, and modernized the banking system. Furthermore, industrialists enjoyed lucrative wartime contracts which allowed them to expand their factories and line their pockets. In the face of inflation and corruption, wartime strikes erupted in both North and South, but government still favored owners over workers and most strikes failed. Yet labor's patience was not unending and major struggles lay ahead.

Many who were inclined to resist labor's challenge felt compelled to reach for an ideology that shifted away from the simple commitment to government by the people and equal opportunity for all expressed by

Lincoln. Drawing on and distorting British naturalist Charles Darwin's theory of evolution, some pro-capitalist intellectuals argued that society involved a struggle for "the survival of the fittest." The rich had proved to be better than the poor, these Social-Darwinist ideologists argued: an elite had risen to the top, economically and politically, because they proved to be more "fit" than the majority of the people. With the "fittest" in charge of the economy, social progress would be realized. The discontented laborers, small farmers, and others with "envious" or "inferior" minds should not be allowed to penalize their superiors—the big businessmen—by in any way imposing limits on their wealth and power. Those religiously inclined offered a Gospel of Wealth which saw poverty as Divine punishment meted out to the sinful, while wealth was God's reward to the virtuous.

There were some, however, who saw things differently. By the early 1880s Frederick Douglass—bitterly disappointed over the betrayal of earlier hopes—observed the "sharp contrast of wealth and poverty" resulting from "one side getting more than its proper share and the other side getting less," commenting that "in some way labor has been defrauded or otherwise denied its due proportion." Douglass's conclusion was similar to that of many labor activists: "As the laborer becomes more intelligent he will develop what capital he already possesses—that is the power to combine and organize for its own protection." A lesson for black and white workers, he felt, should be taken from the earlier antislavery struggle: "Experience demonstrates that there may be a slavery of wages only a little less galling and crushing in its effects than chattel slavery, and that this slavery of wages must go down with the other."

CHAPTER 6

"Gilded Age"

"Get rich; dishonestly if we can; honestly if we must," the great novelist and humorist Mark Twain mockingly wrote of the spirit that triumphed throughout the country, a spirit of "money-fever, sordid ideals, vulgar ambitions, and the sleep that does not refresh." Twain called the post–Civil War period the "Gilded Age" because the glitter of the era covered over widespread corruption. In fact, some historians refer to government generosity to corporations as the period of the "great barbecue," after the nineteenth-century tradition whereby politicians bribed ordinary voters with a big dinner just before election day. For instance, railroads stretching westward were granted miles of land on either side of new lines. Railroads then sold the land to settlers, and charged them ruinous rates to ship or receive goods. The U.S. government sent troops into the West to clear away the native American peoples (the various Indian tribes) who were obstacles to the economic "progress" represented by the expanding corporate-capitalist economy. Back East, however, it turned its eyes as great fortunes were made selling "watered" stock or manipulating the stock market. In 1873, a severe national depression was triggered when financier Jay Cooke went bankrupt due to overextended railroad investments (although in later years he rebuilt his fortune by shifting from banking to mining). The economic liberty of a few was allowed to create misery for millions. The U.S. Constitution defended citizens' rights only against governmental abuse, and not against abuse by corporations. In fact, the Fourteenth Amendment to the Constitution, ostensibly written to protect citizenship rights of ex-slaves, was also purposely worded to expand the rights of corporations! Securing democratic control over the industrial economy would not be an easy task.

National Labor Union

While corporations had a national form, trade-union organizations developed much more slowly. In 1866, workers formed the National Labor Union which focused much of its energies on limiting the work day to eight hours. Boston mechanic Ira Steward played a special role in agitating and educating for reduction of the workday in subsequent years, organizing and winning adherents to the Eight Hour Leagues. Instead of twelve to fourteen hours a day of work, there would be "eight hours for work, eight hours for rest, and eight hours for what we will." It was iron molder William Sylvis, however, who was the moving force behind the NLU.

"I deny that there is an identity of interest between labor and capitalists," Sylvis had explained in 1864. "Capitalists employ labor for the amount of profit realized, and working men labor for the amount of wages received. We find capitalists ever watchful of their interests—ever ready to make everything bend to their desires. Then why should not laborers be equally watchful of their interests—equally ready to take advantage of every circumstance to secure good wages and social elevation?" Sylvis was motivated by a powerful vision of a better life for the working class:

> To secure these blessings, two things are absolutely necessary. We want more time and more money; fewer hours of toil, and more wages for what we do. These wants we will supply, and these evils we will remedy

through the instrumentality of our organizations. We must have a thorough combination of all branches of labor. And then by cooperation we must erect our own workshops, and establish our own stores, and till our own farms, and live in our own houses—in short, we must absolutely control within ourselves the two elements of capital—labor and money. Then we will not only secure a fair standard of wages, but all the profits of our labor.

Disunity continued to plague the ranks of organized labor, however. Many workers in the NLU and in other organizations sought to ban "coolie labor" by preventing the immigration of Chinese workers. (Ironically, while most white unionists viewed Chinese workers as hopelessly docile, it was 5,000 Chinese railroad-track workers who led one of the largest strikes in this country's history against a California firm in 1866.) Also, the NLU's relationship with women workers was quite strained. Only two of thirty national unions (the printers and cigar makers) allowed women members. When feminist and NLU member Susan B. Anthony attempted to recruit women to gain jobs in the printing trades—as strikebreakers—male NLU members who resented her feminism leaped at the opportunity to expel her. On the other hand, the general trend of the NLU was in the direction of overcoming working-class disunity, due to the growing recognition that "an injury to one is an injury to all." Recognizing the importance of international working-class solidarity—because capitalism is a global system, workers of various countries were coming to recognize that they faced similar conditions and often the same adversaries—the NLU established contact with and considered joining the International Workingmen's Association (the European-based "First International" led by Karl Marx). And perhaps most significantly, the NLU closely cooperated with the Colored National Labor Union which was formed in 1869. The fragility of organized labor was demonstrated, however, when the depression of 1873 allowed employers to destroy both the NLU and the CNLU.

Explosions
At times the fight against organized labor took on the quality of outright warfare. A peaceful, if radical, workers' demonstration in New York City's Tompkins Square calling for an end to unemployment and an eight-hour workday in 1874 drew 25,000 men, women, and children but was brutally attacked and dispersed by mounted police. Some workers

were prepared to employ violence as well. In eastern Pennsylvania mining districts during the early 1870s, Irish immigrant miners were accused of fighting back against the most oppressive employers through a violent sort of guerrilla warfare: mines were blown up, mine superintendents were killed, etc. The arrest and hanging of some of the most militant of the workers' leaders (as reflected in the film *The Molly Maguires*) secured a form of law and order that enabled employers to rest more easily—for a short time.

By 1877, workers had endured years of blacklisting, wage cuts, and twelve-to fourteen-hour workdays. In 1877, the Baltimore & Ohio railroad joined with three other major lines and imposed yet another wage cut. On July 16, trainmen in West Virginia struck, and the strike movement quickly spread throughout the country. As the largest and most powerful employer in the United States, for many people railroads symbolized all that was wrong with industrial America. One Pittsburgh iron worker told a mass meeting that "I won't call employers despots, I won't call them tyrants, but the term 'capitalist' is sort of synonymous and will do as well." Local members of the state militia were too sympathetic to the workers to be used in efforts to suppress the uprising, but regiments from the other side of Pennsylvania were brought in to fire into the crowd. More than twenty workers, including three children, were killed, but the city's enraged working people armed themselves and drove the "invaders" back. (After the great strike was over, the federal government strengthened the national guard, placing numerous armories in working-class neighborhoods.)

During the 1877 strike, employers and "respectable society" feared that they were witnessing an American version of the 1871 Paris Commune, where radical and socialist workers had taken over and run the city for several weeks (before being savagely repressed by the forces of upper-class "law and order"). U.S. employers and political leaders responded forcefully to the 1877 strike. Federal troops (some of which had been withdrawn from the South with the selling-out of Reconstruction, and some of which had been used to subdue Indians in the West) were deployed against the rebellious workers. Strikers were driven from the streets of Chicago by artillery, and in cities and towns throughout the country a pro-business version of "law and order" was imposed. But the immense ferment of the 1877 strikes lingered—vivid memories of struggle and solidarity. In St. Louis, for example, black workers on the city's docks had waged a sympathy strike with the rail workers, and when one black striker asked a mass rally "Will you stand with us regardless of color?" the crowd cheered "We will! We will! We will!" While repression broke the strike, workers' rising aspirations for a more just society found new outlets.

Knights of Labor

In the wake of the Great Uprising of 1877, local Labor and Greenback parties grew in strength; advocating the printing of paper money (as in the Civil War) to end the long deflationary period and push back the power of big banking interests, Greenbackers also pushed for major social reforms beneficial to workers and small farmers.*

No less important for the labor movement was the Noble and Holy Order of the Knights of Labor. Formed by Uriah Stephens and others in 1869 as a secret society of tailors, in 1879 the Knights went public, by this time joined by shoe workers, machinists, coal miners, and many others. The Knights accepted all workers except lawyers, politicians, and liquor dealers. They attracted thousands of members: white and black, immigrant and native-born. Stephens's organization was guided by the notion—practically unique on the U.S. social scene—that "the (outside) color of a [membership] candidate shall not debar him from admission; rather let the coloring of his mind and heart be the test," and between 60,000 and 90,000 African Americans became members of the Order.

Women as well as men were active in the organization. "In all our assemblies, local, district, trade and general, woman has an equal voice, when a member, with her brother trade unionist," one female member asserted, and while the Order was hardly free from all male supremacist

---

* Deflation—the increase in the value of the dollar, which meant a decline in prices—especially hit hard the masses of debt-ridden farmers in the post–Civil War years. The inflationary expansion of paper currency ("greenbacks") was seen as helping the small farmer as well as supplying more capital that would stimulate economic growth. This economic growth, it was presumed, would be helpful to manufacturers as well as industrial workers—who were seen (along with the farmers) as "the producing classes," as opposed to the powerful bankers and financiers who preferred a "tight currency." Many of the Greenback reformers made special appeals to workers and the labor movement by connecting the issue of currency reform to pro-labor rhetoric and social reforms. Many labor radicals, especially socialists and advocates of the eight-hour workday, viewed "greenbackism" as a diversion for the workers.

attitudes, it was far ahead of its time. It encouraged women to become members, supported equal pay for equal work among women and men, favored the right to vote for women, and counted women's rights leaders Susan B. Anthony and Elizabeth Cady Stanton among its honored members. Historian Robert Weir has suggested that cultural differences between working-class men and women—with men worried about definitions of "manhood" and women concerned more with a sense of community—resulted in many male members involving themselves more with the Order's rituals while female members "expressed great enthusiasm for dances, debates, socials, songfests, teas and trade fairs." But women and men alike were especially drawn to the organization's radical social idealism.

"We seek to raise the level of wages and reduce the hours of labor; to protect men and women in their occupations, in their lives and limbs, and in their rights as citizens," explained the Knights' executive board in an 1886 statement. "We also seek to secure such legislation as shall tend to prevent the unjust accumulation of wealth, to restrict the power of monopolies and corporations, and to enact such wise and beneficent legislation as shall promote equity and justice, looking to the day when cooperation shall supersede the wage system, and the castes and classes that now divide men shall be forever abolished."

Although the Knights were not immune from the anti-Chinese campaign against "coolie labor" (even as nativist mobs attacked, beat up, and sometimes killed immigrant workers from China), the general trajectory of the Knights of Labor was to include all working people in one big organization under the slogan: "An Injury to One Is an Injury to All." For example, the Knights provided a powerful vehicle for black-white unity. Strongest in the North, the Knights nonetheless attracted both black and white coal miners in Alabama, dockworkers in New Orleans, and tobacco workers in Virginia. In 1885, railroad members of the Knights led a successful strike against one of Jay Gould's railroads. The solidarity that came out of the Knights proved key. Soon more than 700,000 had joined up.

The organization's unique strengths moved it beyond workplace issues to embrace broad social aspirations and community networks of workers. Nonetheless, it was an unwieldy organization. Cooperatives were emphasized, even to the point of expelling trade unionists in the cigar trades in order to sell (below union rates) cooperatively made cigars.

The leadership of the organization—centered around the Grand Master Workman of the "noble and holy order," Terrence V. Powderly—had an expansive social vision, but also fatal impulses toward conservatism and "respectability." Powderly believed railroad tycoon Jay Gould's offers of friendship and "cooperation," and the Knights were inadequately prepared for the vicious counterassault from this man who boasted, "I can hire one half of the working class to kill the other half." In 1886 their organization on the railroads was crushed. In the same period, Southern Knights were viciously race-baited. Responsibility for all forms of labor violence and the most despicable motives were laid at the Knights' door by the powerful pro-business newspapers throughout the country.

AFL and Labor Radicalism

As the Knights were being destroyed by employers and the press, another national labor organization, the American Federation of Labor, was growing. It was chiefly made up of skilled workers, organized into tightly structured craft unions, some of whose leaders had long been active in the labor and socialist movements. (Socialists believed that the economy should be socially owned, democratically controlled, and used to meet the needs of all.) These more durable organizations—focused on improved wages and conditions at the workplace—shared a view of the world stated in the 1886 preamble of the AFL's new constitution: "[A] struggle is going on in all the nations of the civilized world, between the oppressors and the oppressed of all countries, a struggle between the capitalist and the laborer, which grows in intensity from year to year, and will work disastrous results to the toiling millions, if they are not combined for mutual protection and benefit."

The AFL's immediate predecessor (the looser Federation of Organized Trades and Labor Unions, created in 1881) had—under the inspiration of Carpenter's union leader Peter J. McGuire—initiated a nationwide campaign for the eight-hour workday. This demand was essentially a part of workers' struggles for control over their own lives as well as over the labor process which absorbed so much of their energy and time. The campaign included the call for a day of strikes and demonstrations on May 1, 1886. Hundreds of thousands participated throughout the country—but the strongest show of strength was in Chicago, where organized workers from both the craft unions and the Knights shut down workplaces and dominated the city's streets.

Among the leaders of the vibrant and militant Chicago labor move-ment were people—such as German-born August Spies and Texas-born Albert Parsons—who at various times referred to themselves as social-ists, communists, and anarchists. Distrusting politicians and govern-ments, they argued that the working class must free itself through its own efforts, eventually overthrowing capitalism and replacing it with a "cooperative commonwealth" in which—in the words of the *Communist Manifesto*—"the free development of each is the condition for the free development of all." Such stuff was not palatable to Chicago's employers, newspapers, and police force, who made a special target of the radical labor leaders. At a May 4 rally in Haymarket Square, violence erupted when the police moved in to break up the gathering. A bomb was thrown at the police, and the police opened fire on the crowd. A number of policemen and workers were killed. The authorities blamed the bombing on the "Chicago anarchists," whose leaders were arrested and railroaded to the gallows in an unfair trial. Several years too late, Illinois Governor Peter Altgeld pronounced that the Haymarket Martyrs—innocent of the crime with which they were charged—had done little more than argue that the class violence of the time necessitated workers' self-defense.

Outraged by the state-sponsored murder of labor activists, and com-mitted to achieving an eight-hour workday and other rights for labor internationally, workers around the world made May 1 a workers holi-day. Significantly, the other labor holiday—the September Labor Day later preferred by the U.S. government—had also been advanced in 1882 by the originator of May Day, labor radical P. J. McGuire.

Partly in response to the antilabor offensive, there was an upsurge of labor party activity in the late 1880s in various cities. Among the most successful efforts was that of the United Labor Party in New York—supported by the unions, various reformers, and socialists—which ran reformer Henry George for mayor in 1887. George narrowly missed winning (some suggest that the election was stolen by the Democratic Party machine), with Republican mayoral candidate Theodore Roosevelt coming in a distant third. These efforts soon evaporated, however, as factional differences erupted between the labor parties' various constitu-ents, and also because of fears that a fragmentation of workers between the Democrats and Republicans would be further complicated by a third Labor Party division.

And yet labor radicalism did not evaporate. In his 1893 pamphlet *What Does Labor Want?* AFL President Samuel Gompers expressed the views of many in emphasizing "the separation of the capitalistic class from the great laboring mass," adding that "the capitalist class had its origins in force and fraud," and that "this class of parasites devours incomes derived from many sources, from the stunted babies employed in the mills, mines and factories to the lessees of the gambling halls and the profits of fashionable brothels; from the lands which the labor of others had made valuable; from the royalties on coal and other miners beneath the surface and from rent of houses above the surface." In opposition to this, Gompers believed that the working class was entitled to "the earth and the fullness thereof. There is nothing too precious, there is nothing too beautiful, too lofty, too ennobling, unless it is within the scope and comprehension of labor's aspirations and wants."

Gompers viewed "true trade unionists" as those "who recognize the vital, logical extension, growth, and development of all unions of all trades and callings, and who strive for the unity, federation, cooperation, fraternity, and solidarity of all organized wage-earners; who can and do subordinate self for the common good and always strive for the common uplift; who decline to limit the sphere of their activity by any dogma, doctrine, or ism." The primary need—independent of any radical ideology—was to build strong organizations of workers in the workplaces that could draw the diverse employees into a unified effort that would compel employers to give better wages, shorter hours, and improved working conditions. When asked what the labor movement wanted, Gompers once replied simply: "More." His view—from the 1880s until his death in the 1920s—was eloquently expressed in an early speech:

> If a workingman gets a dollar and a half for ten hours' work, he lives up to that standard of a dollar and a half, and he knows that a dollar seventy-five would improve his standard of living and he naturally strives to get that dollar and seventy-five. After that he wants two dollars and more time for leisure, and he struggles to get it. Not satisfied with two dollars he wants more; not only two and a quarter, but a nine-hour workday. And so he will keep on getting more and more until he gets it all or the full value of all he produces.

Moderation and Militancy

As time went on, however, the AFL came to represent a relatively conservative form of trade unionism. The skills and social standing of most of its members allowed them to bargain with employers about wages and working conditions. The ability of their unions to survive in the face of economic fluctuations and employer hostility was impressive, but the membership of the craft unions tended to be restricted to white males who had been born in the United States or who had immigrated years before. What's more, presumably "utopian" ventures, like independent labor politics or cooperatives or socialist strategies, were abandoned in favor of what AFL President Gompers and others called "pure and simple unionism," which—Gompers explained—saw the trade union itself as "the natural organization of wage workers to secure their present material and practical improvement and to achieve their final emancipation." Although sometimes still tipping his hat to abstract socialist ideals, Gompers also referred to trade unions in nonradical terms as "the business organization of the wage earners to attend to the business of the wage earners," and was soon denouncing socialists for seeking "to allure our movement into such a vortex of complications and capture our movement as a tail to their political kite." He abandoned his earlier anticapitalist rhetoric and went out of his way to show employers and mainstream politicians that he was now hostile to left-wing ideologies. Yet many AFL members remained socialists, and their 1894 resolution calling for the national ownership of all industries was only narrowly defeated. Daniel DeLeon, doctrinaire chieftain of the Socialist Labor Party, castigated the AFL leaders as "labor lieutenants of capitalism." DeLeon sought to create a rival Socialist Trades and Labor Alliance, but it was never a serious alternative to Gompers's federation and AFL stalwarts (including many socialists) denounced it as "dual unionism."

Under Gompers and his cothinkers, however, the House of Labor came to have little room for political radicals, or for blacks and other people of color, or most immigrants from southern or eastern Europe. In the five decades from 1870 to 1920, wave upon wave of immigrant labor inundated industrializing America, helping to decompose and recompose the U.S. working class in ways that disrupted and fragmented labor organization and class consciousness, and many in the AFL viewed this mass of newcomers as an unorganizable threat to hard-won union gains. While women of all nationalities were also excluded from many unions and labor struggles, there were some who refused to be excluded from the fight for social justice. There was the almost unstoppable Leonora O'Reilley, who organized for the Knights of Labor, the AFL's garment workers, and later the Women's Trade Union League. And there was the tough-as-nails but grandmotherly organizer for the United Mine Workers, "Mother" Mary Jones, exulting that "women in the industrial field have begun to awaken to their condition of slavery . . . and they gave battle fearlessly. . . . Never can a complete victory be won until the woman awakens to her condition."

As it turned out, neither maleness nor skill nor white skin nor "respectability" would necessarily protect AFL members from the greed of employers. In 1892, Andrew Carnegie attempted to introduce new technology that would weaken craft workers' control over the Homestead, Pennsylvania steel mill. He and his top manager, Henry Clay Frick, then used a lockout to break the union altogether. But the unionized skilled workers had gathered the support of the local government and most of the unskilled, largely Slavic workforce. In a violent and determined struggle, the Amalgamated Association of Iron and Steel Workers, in alliance with the less skilled non-unionized workers and the entire community of Homestead, succeeded in repulsing several hundred armed Pinkerton guards hired to ensure operationsof the steel works on a non-union basis. Seven workers and three Pinkertons were killed, and many others injured in the "Battle of Homestead." The Pennsylvania militia then did the job of breaking the workers' struggle. Labor's defeat had a devastating impact on the quality of life, the dignity, and the democratic rights of the working class. Visiting Homestead a year later, the noted writer Hamlin Garland observed that it was "as squalid and unlovely as could well be imagined, and the people were mainly of the discouraged and sullen type to be found everywhere where labor passes into the brutalizing stage of severity," adding: "Such towns are sown thickly over the hill-lands of Pennsylvania." Victorious Carnegie's profits soared, protected by a spy system that fingered and blacklisted unionists. By the early 1900s, Mother Jones succinctly characterized the political impact of the economic dictatorship: "The class that owns the [industrial] machine owns the government, it owns the governors, it owns the courts and it owns the public officials all along the line."

The craft organization of the AFL worked well in the building trades. There, craft unionists could impose work rules and raise wages. Union workers in other trades bought union-made products (such as cigars) and boycotted non-union products or those built with prison labor, calling on all workers to buy only "union label" products. But by the late nineteenth and early twentieth centuries the strategy involving a different union for each job or "craft" was being outflanked in modern industries which combined new technologies and mass production techniques that undermined the power of skilled workers and blurred distinctions between skilled and unskilled. A few unions, such as the United Mine Workers, attempted to organize all the employees in an industry, regardless of their job. Similar efforts were soon made in the garment industry as well.

One of the most dramatic examples of intercraft solidarity came in the early 1890s when over 150,000 railroad workers joined the American Railway Union led by Eugene Victor Debs. Industrial organization and solidarity bested the Great Northern line in 1894. Later that year, ARU members supported the strike of workers who built Pullman railroad cars. ARU members refused to couple any Pullman cars to trains, and half a million railroad workers were idled. Railroad companies got a federal judge to issue an injunction effectively outlawing the ARU boycott of Pullman cars. Then the government placed U.S. mail onto Pullman cars. Debs and other unionists were jailed while federal troops attacked strikers. Fearful of risking its own existence in this mighty confrontation, the AFL refused to support the ARU and the boycott, resulting in the collapse of the strike and the rail union.

Robber Barons and Economic Expansionism

The Homestead and Pullman strikes were reflections of larger developments in U.S. society, especially in the economy. The rise of big business corporations made possible the immense reorganization, the enlarged scale, the far-reaching interconnection of economic enterprises that greatly raised efficiency and productivity. New technology and work methods were developed to enhance the employers' control of the labor process at the workplace—often by utilizing "scientific management" methods pioneered by Frederick W. Taylor. This broke down workers' skills, subordinated them to the will of tough-minded corporation managers, speeded up their work, and helped to break their unions and cut their wages.

At the same time, the growth of industry meant more jobs, lower prices for consumer goods, and a growing array of products that profoundly altered and seemed to improve Americans' way of life—and this, in turn, attracted new waves of immigrants seeking a better life than they could find in Ireland, in southern and eastern Europe, in Asia, in Mexico, etc. Yet the new economic developments destroyed smaller businesses, brought small farmers to the brink of ruin thanks to the callous policies of banks and big corporations that dominated the agricultural sectors of the economy. And "industrial progress" made workers more vulnerable than ever to the power of their employers. The economic leaders of the corporate economy—people like Morgan and Mellon in banking, Rockefeller in oil and coal, Carnegie and Frick in steel, Gould and Hill in rail, Swift and Armour in meatpacking, etc.—were seen as "robber barons" by the many who were victimized as a result of their spectacular profiteering.

In 1890, the richest 9 percent of the population owned 71 percent of the nation's wealth (with the .03 percent who were millionaires enjoying 20 percent). A 39 percent middle layer of the population had 24 percent of the wealth, and the bottom 52 percent of the population had only 5 percent of the wealth. An indignant South Dakota Senator R. F. Pettigrew (a maverick Republican) commented that this translated politically into "rule by and for the rich." It also translated into many hardships for the majority of the people.

Sometimes the quest for profits through rising productivity resulted in overproduction—a glut on the market of products which couldn't be sold, resulting in large-scale business failures and massive unemployment: economic depression. While such depressions were disasters for most of the population, they enabled the more powerful corporations to become more dominant forces in the economy, with the elimination of their less efficient competitors. More than this, as we have seen, the economic power translated into political power, and the big corporations became profoundly influential at all levels of government and in both major political parties. Denouncing such "plutocracy" (rule by the rich), radicalized small farmers spearheaded the Populist movement—which attracted many workers and some unions (the Knights of Labor, the ARU, and others)—in an effort to end the domination of big business and give power to America's laboring majority. Populists first won electoral successes through their own party, then put all their eggs into the basket of the Democratic Party—whose presidential campaign of William Jennings Bryan was crushed in 1896 by the much more powerful, hugely financed campaign of Republican William McKinley. Over the next few decades, the bulk of small farmers who had made up the main Populist base were eliminated as an independent economic and political force.

Business and political leaders recognized, however, that general economic prosperity had to be provided if the sort of discontent represented by labor radicals and Populists was to be kept under control. Economic expansion overseas—to secure more markets for U.S. goods, plentiful raw materials for U.S. industries, and new investment opportunities for U.S. businessmen—was seen as one of the keys to economic prosperity in the United States. The consequence was a U.S. foreign policy designed to advance such economic goals, and intensified "patriotic" campaigns to support the military muscle sometimes needed to back all of this up.

An early result was what McKinley's secretary of the navy (and later his vice president and his presidential successor) Theodore Roosevelt termed a "splendid little war" against Spain, to push this antiquated rival out of the way in the Caribbean and the Philippines. With relatively little loss of U.S. lives, Cuba was "liberated" from Spanish rule and placed under U.S. "protection," and Puerto Rico became an outright colony. The Philippines—after U.S. soldiers went on to fight a brutal four-year "dirty war" to prevent Filipinos from establishing the first republic in Asia—also became a U.S. possession.

Some trade unionists (including the AFL's Samuel Gompers) joined with other reformers to form an "Anti-Imperialist League" in opposition to such policies—but nothing could prevent the inexorable economic expansionism. As in earlier "Indian wars," most of the benefits went to land speculators and corporations that established sugar and pineapple plantations. U.S. leaders were not inclined, however, to build a colonial empire. They preferred, through a judicious mix of "dollar diplomacy" and "gunboat diplomacy," to maintain an "Open Door" policy that would give American businesses access to markets, resources, and investment opportunities in a variety of foreign climes.

CHAPTER 7

Rainbow Working Class

The working class of the United States is one of the most diverse in the entire world. "This is not a nation but a teeming nation of nations," wrote the poet Walt Whitman. Incensed over the common assertion that "the essential faith of America came into being in Puritan New England," radical journalist Louis Adamic responded:

> There is "essential faith of America" also in the labor of the Irish and Chinese railroad builders, the mixed-strain Paul Bunyan work gangs in the North Woods, the Cornish and Montenegrin copper miners of Keewenaw and Butte, the Finnish iron miners of Ishpeming, the men of many immigrant stocks who have shoveled the ore of the Mesabi Range into the boats on Lake Superior, the Slavic and Lithuanian steelworkers of Pittsburgh and Gary, the Jewish and Italian garment people of Manhattan, the Russian and Italian sandhogs under the Hudson River, the Scandinavian and German farm-pioneers in the Middle West, the dark cotton pickers of the South . . . (Adamic 1945)

The question naturally arises as to how and why the United States came to have such an extremely diverse population. "The coming of peoples to this continent, voluntarily or in chains, is at the very center of our historical process," Adamic pointed out. "It is a main constituent of America." To a large extent, the first Americans—the peoples who were called "Indians"—were the most tragic victims of this process, even as they heroically and desperately resisted their own destruction, even as essential elements of their own cultures became essential elements of the larger American culture, even as some of the survivors became part of the labor force and labor movement of the United States. There were also Mexicans—blended from Indian and Spanish ancestries—who involuntarily found themselves part of the United States, and second-class

citizens at best, after the United States conquered and absorbed part of their country (California, Utah, Nevada, Arizona, New Mexico, Texas) through the Mexican War of 1846–1848.

The fact remains, as Adamic noted, that the United States involved a "coming of peoples" to the new land: thirty-eight million immigrants entering the country between 1820 and 1940, though most of these came in the period between the Civil War and World War I (1865–1914)— over 27 million people. The greatest proportion of these came from Europe, and before 1880 about 85 percent of the European immigrants came from northern and western Europe (the British Isles, Scandinavia, Germany)—by far the largest concentrations being German and Irish. After 1880 these areas represented less than 20 percent of the "new immigration," which now predominantly came from eastern and southern Europe—from lands claimed by the German kaiser, as well as from the Austro-Hungarian and Russian empires (including what are now Austria, Hungary, Poland, Bulgaria, Rumania, the Czech and Slovak republics, the Ukraine, Russia, etc.), the ethnic patchwork of the former Yugoslavia, plus Italy, Greece, and other Mediterranean countries. The same factors influencing European immigration also generated a growing influx from Asia—China, Japan, the Philippines—as well as newcomers traveling up from Mexico and (a little later) the Caribbean.

While the quest for political and religious liberties influenced some of those coming to the United States, a more widespread influence was an economic "push-pull" factor. Due to the spread of industrial capitalism throughout Europe (first in the north and west, later in the south and east), dramatic changes in population growth and agricultural economies pushed increasing numbers of people out of rural villages and into urban and industrial areas. One of the most dynamically industrializing areas in the world was the United States, where commodity production increased 54 percent between 1869 and 1899. In this period there was a labor shortage in the United States. Investigators of the U.S. Immigration Commission, asking employers why they employed immigrants, were told that it was necessary "either to employ immigrant labor or delay industrial advancement."

In fact, American industrialists didn't simply accept immigrants as employees—they actively encouraged massive immigration. Not only did they need more laborers in general, but they were especially attracted to the special uses to which they could put the immigrants. Historian John Higham has pointed out that "the immigrant derived not only from a more or less alien culture but also from mean, impoverished circumstances. Entering the American economy on its lowest rungs, he commonly began by accepting wages and enduring conditions which Americanized employees scorned."

In addition to this, many industrialists felt that ethnic divisions among their workers made it easier to control the work force. As one steel mill superintendent in Pennsylvania commented in 1875: "My experience has shown that Germans and Irish, Swedes and what I denominate 'Buckwheats'—young American country boys, judiciously mixed, make the most honest and tractable force you can find." Historian Ronald Takaki documents similar patterns in the West—pitting Chinese and Irish railroad workers against each other in Colorado, and encouraging in Hawaii and California fierce ethnic rivalries among Japanese and Filipino agricultural workers. Especially beginning with World War I (but also continuing through the Great Depression and accelerating during World War II), the economic "push-pull" factors drew African Americans in massive numbers, as well as growing numbers of Southern whites (denigrated as "rednecks" and "hillbillies") to Northern urban and industrial areas, adding new elements to the often explosive working-class competition.

A racially and ethnically fragmented working class was a hallmark of U.S. labor, involving "a recurrent tension . . . between native [workers] and immigrant men and women fresh to the factory," in the words of labor historian Herbert Gutman. "That state of tension was regularly revitalized by the migration of diverse . . . peoples into an industrializing or a fully industrialized society." Racism and ethnic bigotry flourished within the divided working class, as earlier immigrants and their children struggled to maintain their precarious "privileges." Some had succeeded in building craft unions, gaining a minimum of economic security only after bitter struggles. Their achievements could be quickly eroded by the influx of any new workers who might be willing to work harder for less money. Many union locals became ethnic enclaves—for native-born Anglo-Saxon Protestants in one place, for the Irish somewhere else, for "Germans only" here, for "Poles only" there, and so on. The strangeness of different customs, languages, accents, even something so essential as a person's skin and hair—all added to the fear and hatred that divided the various workers. Interethnic rivalry as well as nativist bigotry flourished.

"Here I am with these Hunkies," complained one steelworker (making derogatory reference to eastern Europeans). "They don't seem like men to me hardly. They can't talk United States. You tell them something and they just look and say, 'Me no fustay, me no fustay,' that's all you get out of 'em." Another steelworker complained about "a crowd of Negroes and Syrians" working in one mill, adding: "It is no place for a man with a white man's heart to be. The Negroes and foreigners are coarse, vulgar and brutal in their acts and conversation." Another, speaking about jobs in the blast furnace, commented that "only Hunkies work on those jobs, they're too damn dirty and too damn hot for a white man." Indeed, many new immigrants from Europe, beginning with the Irish in the 1840s and going on down to the new waves of southern and eastern Europeans in the early 1900s, aggressively sought to emphasize their own "whiteness" that was supposed to bring them rights and privileges not to be accorded to people of color (African Americans first of all, but also the "yellow peril" from Asia, as well as Mexicans and Puerto Ricans and native American "Indians").

Sometimes these divisions were at least partly overcome. There are accounts from the early 1900s of German and Irish trade-union organizers in Chicago's meatpacking industry laboring successfully to include and "Americanize" Poles, Slovaks, Lithuanians, and Czechs as part of the same multicultural, multilingual organization, and of an Irish American union organizer explaining that what "association together and industrial necessity have shown is that, however it may go against the grain, we must admit that common interests and brotherhood must include the Irish and the Sheeny"—(the latter term being a derogatory word for "Jew"). While employers sought to use African Americans as strikebreakers in the stockyards, the reaction of union leaders was to include black workers in the same union—and with the same rights—as white workers. "We didn't want any Jim Crow situation out there," explained Chicago Federation of Labor President John Fitzpatrick. There are accounts of interethnic solidarity and black-white unity—again born out of brutal necessity—within the locals, stretching from Illinois to Alabama, of the United Mine Workers of America from the 1890s through the early 1900s. Although there were still cases of black union members not being welcome in some union mines, it is also true that the UMW had thousands of black members, a number of whom held union office even in some majority-white locals. There are accounts of a militant 1919 strike of plantation workers in Hawaii embracing Filipinos, Japanese, Spanish, Portuguese, and Chinese. There is this remarkable account, offered by Herbert Gutman, of workers in the silver mines of Virginia City, Nevada:

> The calendar of the social life of Virginia City miners in 1875 reveals their rich cultural diversity. It began New Year's Day with Germans singing and dancing at their Athletic Hall and the French and Italians joining together at Gregoire's Saloon. It continued through that day with a sixteen-piece Cornish orchestra and the English choral society. During the first part of February, the town's Chinese celebrated their New Year and the Italian and Irish benevolent societies had their annual meetings, so that Emmet's Irish guard mixed with Oriental celebrants on the town's streets. A similar conjoining of nationalities could be found at most any time of the year. In August, the Scots celebrated Robert Burns's birthday with a gathering of the clans, and bagpipe music mixed with fortnightly public concerts given by Professor Varney's German band, the players of Emmet's guard, the Cornish orchestra, and the Italian opera company. By month's end, the Miner's Union Hall was converted into a Polish synagogue for Rosh Hashanah and Yom Kippur, Mexicans celebrated their national independence, and a Canadian relief society

met. Yet this whirlwind review of the cultural calendar of Virginia City remains incomplete because it does not mention the powerful industrial union established by the diverse and heterogeneous laboring population. The union they formed in 1863 served as a model for workers over the entire Far West, and the introduction of its constitution was sworn to and signed by new members over the entire mining region.

> In view of the existing evils which the Miners have to endure from the tyrannical oppressive power of Capital, it has become necessary to protest, and to elevate our social condition and maintain a position in society. . . . We should cultivate an acquaintance with our fellows in order that we may be the better enabled to form an undivided opposition to acts of "tyranny." . . . We . . . have resolved to form an association . . . , for without Union we are powerless, with it we are powerful;—and there is no power that can be wielded by Capital or position but which we may boldly defy,—For united we possess strength, let us act justly and fear not.

> Cultural diversity and even conflict did not prevent the formation of this union, which remained powerful in the region. (Gutman 1987)

The fact remains, however, that this was highly unusual through most of the history of the U.S. working class, which was marked by fragmentation and ghettoization, exclusion and ethnocentrism, and the most ignorant, vicious, and often violent anti-black, anti-Asian, anti-Mexican, anti-immigrant bigotry. This characterized much of the labor movement's "mainstream" through the nineteenth and early twentieth centuries. Formally the AFL opposed exclusion of workers on the basis of race, creed, color, or ethnic background—but in fact it was common practice, often apologized for and justified by the AFL leaders themselves. African American workers found that, regardless of skill, they were by and large relegated to the most menial jobs by employers, and many "white" workers made it clear that they wanted it that way. Sometimes the only way that black or immigrant workers could get a decent job was by scabbing on more privileged workers who were on strike. It took some workers a long time to learn the *practicality* of the egalitarianism and solidarity that had at least been partially achieved by meatpackers, coal miners, plantation workers, and silver miners.

The diversity of the working class also found reflection in many creeds—religious and secular—to which the varied inhabitants of this dynamic country adhered. Often priests, ministers, and rabbis were hostile to efforts to improve the world because these were felt to be corrupting diversions from spiritual priorities. Clergymen often attacked efforts of organized labor to challenge the power of the wealthy, who were known to make generous financial contributions to the work of responsible spiritual leaders. There were many others, however, who embraced the cause of labor. Traditions developed of Catholic "labor priests," Protestant ministers who envisioned a labor-based "kingdom of God," and socially conscious rabbis who repeated Hillel's militant injunction: "If I am not for myself, who will be for me? If I am for myself alone, what am I? If not now, when?"

Differing creeds had a potential for dividing workers. Catholic and Protestant workers literally fought pitched battles in the 1840s, and for a number of years the Order of United American Mechanics labored to expose and combat the Catholic "threat." Animosities among the various Protestant sects and between different currents of Catholicism also caused many workers to look down on and draw back from each other. Many Christian workers assumed Jews to be "bankers, millionaires, exploiters, bloodsuckers," and some were astonished when their union organizer, Rosa Pesotta, explaining that she was Jewish, emphasized: "I'm a wage earner, like yourselves; and there are millions like me in the United States who work for a living." Other targets of fierce animosity were the "secular humanists" who were freethinkers, atheists, Marxists, anarchists (yet all of these also proved perfectly capable of developing their own internal divisions,* as well as bigotry toward those who believed differently from themselves). Such dynamics also fragmented the labor movement in a variety of ways over the years.

Here, too, however, it is sometimes the case that what the Irish labor organizer referred to as "association together with industrial necessity" caused the destructive animosities to give way to toleration, mutual

---

* Oscar Ameringer, an old-time socialist intimately involved in the labor movement, observed that in the 1920s and 1930s "the war between the [left-wing] sects of irate upheavers is far more savage than that between capital and labor," going on to lament: "Old friends and comrades assail one another's character and bloody one another's noses over policies and tactics the correctness of which only trial and error can prove or disprove."

respect, even a recognition that among all there was potentially a common ground of belief: a valuing of each individual, a conviction that we each have some responsibility for ourselves and for each other, a commitment to a just community for all people in the vast and infinitely complex and wondrous mystery of existence.

CHAPTER 8
Progressive Era

By the mid-1890s, the United States was the leading manufacturing nation in the world, and by 1900 it had entered the ranks of the major powers in world politics. And yet, the tremendous industrial development that had made this possible created immense social problems which worried some of the more farsighted business and political leaders. There were more and more exposures of and protests against a vast accumulation of evils and injustices: unsafe and unsanitary workplaces and communities, outright political corruption on an unprecedented scale, the enhancement of big business profits through large-scale environmental destruction, generalized fraud and cheating at the public expense, the widespread adulteration and pollution of consumer goods, innumerable and unavoidable manifestations of poverty side-by-side with conspicuous consumption by the wealthy, shocking realities of child labor, etc. Theodore Roosevelt favored the growth of big corporations and what he viewed as their positive contributions, but fretted: "I do not like the social conditions at present. The dull, purblind folly of the very rich men, their greed and arrogance . . . and the corruption in business and politics, have tended to produce a very unhealthy condition of excitement and irritation in the popular mind, which shows itself in the great increase in the socialistic propaganda."

REFORMERS AND SOCIALISTS

Such people concluded that if "progress" was to mean change for the better, then the government would have to play a more active role in society. Mainstream Progressive politicians such as the Republican Roosevelt and the Democrat Woodrow Wilson (elected president in 1912) rejected the old-time laissez-faire economic policies, favoring

instead bold government intervention in the economy. They didn't want to overthrow the power of the big corporations, but instead to set limits on and establish regulations for that power. At the same time, they favored major social reforms to eliminate some of the worst of the problems created by the previous decades of industrialization. They even adopted a policy of encouraging the more "responsible" and moderate union leaders—such as the AFL's Samuel Gompers—who would help advance such reforms while at the same time drawing workers away from socialists and other radicals.

Nonetheless, there was great ferment, and movements for a variety of social reforms proliferated. Pro-labor activists found that it was possible to push forward an agenda that would benefit the working class in a variety of ways. Advocates of women's rights focused especially on securing the right to vote for the female half of the population. Advocates of African American rights mounted antilynching campaigns in the South and pushed for equality before the law throughout the country. Middle-class reformers reached out for an alliance with the labor movement to bring about political reforms—direct election of senators, the right of referendum and recall, etc.—that presumably would make democracy more of a reality.

Some of the more radical Progressives—such as Wisconsin's Republican governor and then senator "Fighting Bob" LaFollette—were especially militant in their call for political and social reforms, and in their pro-labor attitudes, and (unlike Roosevelt and Wilson) they *did* want to break the power of big business corporations for the benefit of workers, farmers, and small business people.

The furthest left fringe of Progressivism, however, was occupied by those attracted to the Socialist Party of America. Marxist ideas that had influenced many labor radicals down through the years were blended, among these Progressive-era leftists, with other influences as well. There was the influence of the best-selling utopian novel *Looking Backward*, whose author Edward Bellamy noted that "true and humane men and women of every degree are in a mood of exasperation, verging on absolute revolt, against social conditions that reduce life to a brutal struggle for existence." There was the influence of the Social Gospel of such radical Christians as Rev. Walter Rauschenbusch, who insisted that "the force of the religious spirit should be bent toward asserting the supremacy of life over property," and that "it is unchristian to regard human life as a mere instrument for the production of wealth." And there were influential leftist renderings of John Dewey's pragmatic philosophy (according to William English Walling, "the great social revolution as it appears in the world of thought") which insisted, as Dewey put it, on the need for concentrating "all the instrumentalities of the social arts, of law, of education, economics and political science upon the construction of intelligent methods of improving the common lot."

Socialists—led by former American Railway Union leader Eugene V. Debs—won a base of members and supporters numbering in the hundreds of thousands, especially among workers, and even wider influence throughout society, becoming a primary force for social reform, an inclusive and militant trade unionism, and expanding democracy. Debs became widely known and loved for the personal warmth and expansive idealism with which he explained his party's program: "The Socialist Party as the party of the exploited workers in the mills and mines, on the railways and on the farms, the workers of both sexes and all races and colors, the working class in a word, constituting a great majority of the people and in fact THE PEOPLE, demands that the nation's industries shall be taken over by the nation and that the nation's workers shall operate them for the benefit of the whole people."

Many remarkable people were drawn to this movement, such as the pioneering social worker Florence Kelley, the black scholar W. E. B. Du Bois who led the newly formed National Association for the Advancement of Colored People (NAACP), best-selling writers Jack London and Upton Sinclair, the poet Carl Sandburg, and others. There was the daughter of the Kansas working class Kate Richards O'Hare, who had "teased, coaxed and cajoled the men" into letting her become a skilled machinist, and then went on to become one of the Socialist Party's leading agitators: "The working class is not pleased with the actual administration of things. Their interests are not served. Actual democracy has not been practiced." As with many Socialists, her ideals were flavored by her earlier religious upbringing, as she called for "co-operation instead of competition, a world where greed, and vice, and avarice have been replaced by brotherhood, and justice and humanity." An outspoken advocate of women's suffrage, she saw most women as part of the working-class majority: "We want to use our ballot to peacefully bring about the social revolution which shall eliminate wage slavery and establish the collective ownership and democratic control of the collectively owned means of life."

A significant force throughout the twentieth century's first two decades, the Socialist Party of America polled 6 percent of the total presidential vote (with Debs as the candidate) in 1912, actually electing 1,200 candidates in 340 municipalities throughout the country, including 79 mayors in 24 states. There were hundreds of thousands—perhaps millions—of readers for the party's 323 English and foreign-language daily, weekly, and monthly periodicals—the nationally distributed *Appeal to Reason* alone having a weekly circulation of more than 761,000. With 5,000 local branches throughout the country, the party had a dues-paying membership of about 120,000. Some of the most dedicated activists in the labor movement were identified with it. "Within the short period of twelve years the Socialist Party has grown from a state of insignificance to the importance of a serious factor in the national life of the United States," commented labor lawyer Morris Hillquit, who concluded with an optimistic flourish: "It is safe to predict that in another dozen years it will contend with the old parties for political supremacy."

Industrial Workers of the World

It has been estimated that about one-third of the AFL was Socialist in this period, but many Socialists joined with other militant workers to establish a radically new labor organization in 1905, the Industrial Workers of the World. IWW leader "Big Bill" Haywood—coming to the organization from the Western Federation of Miners—described its founding meeting in Chicago as the "constitutional convention of the working class." Disgusted with the moderation and exclusiveness of the AFL, the IWW pledged to organize the entire working class on an industrial basis regardless of race, sex, or occupation into "One Big Union." Nicknamed the "Wobblies," these radical labor activists sought to create a revolutionary union that would fight for immediate gains as steps designed to lead eventually (preferably sooner than later) to a general strike by the entire working class that would bring the entire capitalist economy and government to an absolute halt. With power in the hands of the working-class majority, the economy would then be owned, organized, and run by and for the working class.

AFL leaders accused these labor radicals of "dual unionism," a cardinal sin in many labor circles, while the Wobblies criticized the AFL for siding with the bosses against workers who were ready to struggle under the IWW banner. And many workers responded to the radicals' efforts.

The Wobblies reached out to timber workers on the West Coast, harvest hands on the Great Plains, textile workers in New England, steelworkers in the Midwest, and many more. One Wobbly was an immigrant from the Philippines named Philip Vera Cruz, who later helped to organize the United Farm Workers. The IWW organized black and white timber workers in a united struggle in Louisiana. The organization proved willing and able to organize the "unorganizable," such as the thousands of immigrant textile workers who struck in Lawrence, Massachusetts in 1912, where the eloquent Wobbly orator Elizabeth Gurley Flynn joined with other skilled organizers such as Arturo Giovannitti and Carlo Tresca to mobilize workers and their families, leading them to victory. Flynn explained the IWW conception of "a labor victory" by insisting that strikes must help workers "gain economic advantage, but they must also gain revolutionary spirit, in order to achieve a complete victory." She elaborated:

For workers to gain a few more cents a day, a few minutes less a day, and go back to work with the same psychology, the same attitude toward society is to have achieved a temporary gain and not a lasting victory. For workers to go back with a class-conscious spirit, with an organized and determined attitude toward society means that even if they have made no economic gain they have the possibility of gaining in the future. In other words, a labor victory must be economic and it must be revolutionizing. Otherwise it is not complete.

In his opening remarks at the founding convention of the IWW, proclaiming the intention of "emancipation of the working class from the slave bondage of capitalism," militant leader "Big Bill" Haywood castigated the AFL for failing to represent the entire working class, noting that "there are organizations affiliated . . . with the A.F. of L. which in their constitution and by-laws prohibit the initiation or conferring of the obligation on a colored man; that prohibit the conferring of the obligation on foreigners. What we want to establish at this time is a labor organization that will open wide its doors to every man that earns his livelihood either by brain or muscle." Like the organization he led, Haywood seemed to embrace the entire working class. "He actually loved to spend time with the workers, to talk with their women and children," recalled tough-minded anarchist Carlo Tresca of the hulking, battle-scarred organizer. "He went to supper with strikers nearly every night. . . . He would sleep in the houses of Italians, Syrians, Irish, Poles, Letts. People were all brothers to him."

Such feelings were translated into practical organizational realities. From 1913 to the early 1920s, for example, a largely immigrant and black local of the IWW controlled Philadelphia's docks, led by Ben Fletcher, an African American. "The organized labor movement has not begun to become a contender for its place in the sun, until every man, woman and child in industry is eligible to be identified with its cause, regardless of race, color or creed," Fletcher argued in 1923. Noting that "organized labor for the most part be it radical or conservative, thinks in terms of the white race," he emphasized that this would be changed only when black workers themselves organized "to generate a force which when necessary could have rendered low the dragon head of race prejudice, whenever and wherever it raised its head." The militant union he led showed how this could be done, leading to black-white unity and consequent gains for all workers.

The Wobblies became well-known for the many songs they produced and popularized. Swedish immigrant Joe Hill—with the clever and biting humor of such compositions as "Casey Jones" and "The Preacher and the Slave"—was one of the most popular of the agitating songwriters, even more so after his 1915 martyrdom, but the most famous IWW musical contribution to the labor movement was the stirring anthem "Solidarity Forever," which became known by millions of workers for more than eight decades after 1915, when it was written by Ralph Chaplin:

> When the Union's inspiration through the workers blood shall run,
> There can be no power greater anywhere beneath the sun.
> Yet what force on earth is weaker than the feeble strength of one?
> But the Union makes us strong.
>
> Solidarity forever, Solidarity forever, Solidarity forever,
> For the Union makes us strong.
>
> They have taken untold millions that they never toiled to earn,
> But without our brain and muscle not a single wheel can turn,
> We can break their haughty power, gain our freedom when we learn
> That the Union makes us strong.
>
> Solidarity forever, Solidarity forever, Solidarity forever,
> For the Union makes us strong.
>
> In our hands is placed a power greater than their hoarded gold,
> Greater than the might of armies magnified a thousandfold.
> We can bring to birth a new world from the ashes of the old.
> For the Union makes us strong.
>
> Solidarity forever, Solidarity forever, Solidarity forever,
> For the Union makes us strong.

One Wobbly organizer, James P. Cannon, critically reflected on strengths and weaknesses of the organization years later. The strengths continued to revitalize and influence the labor and radical movements for many decades after the Wobblies ceased to be a significant force. The weaknesses, he felt, could be traced to the mixing together of two different functions: that of a trade union with that of a revolutionary party. For the core of militant working-class activists drawn to its banner, the IWW became "their one all-sufficient organization—their union and their party; their social center; their home; their family; their school;

and in a manner of speaking, their religion, without the supernatural trappings—the faith they lived by." Yet this undercut the organization's ability to function as an effective trade union. While calling for strong industrial unions in the new mass-production industries, "in all the most militant years of the IWW the best it could accomplish in modern mass production industry were localized strikes, nearly all of which were defeated. The victorious Lawrence strike of 1912, which established the national fame of the IWW, was the glorious exception. But no stable and permanent union organization was ever maintained anywhere in the East for any length of time—not even in Lawrence." Seeking to maintain ongoing militancy at the workplace, without signing any contract with the employer that would limit the workers' right to strike any time they saw fit, undermined the Wobblies' ability to secure stable union recognition. (No less decisive in the eventual defeat of the IWW, of course, was the severe repression by employers' private "security" forces, as well as by—at various times—local, state, and national governments.)

Cannon, a lifelong revolutionary socialist, valued highly the IWW "as an organization of revolutionists, united not simply by the immediate economic interests which bind all workers together in a union, but by doctrine and program" proclaiming—in the words of the IWW 1908 constitutional preamble—that "the working class and the employing class have nothing in common" and that "between these two classes a struggle must go on until the workers of the world organize as a class, take possession of the earth and the machinery of production, and abolish the wage system." Yet while revolutionaries can help to build strong and effective unions to advance the workers' interests, such an organization of revolutionaries—Cannon concluded—cannot itself function as a trade union, which must include masses of workers, many of whom may not (at least for some time) understand or agree with the revolutionary program.

The Coming of the First World War

The IWW by no means had a monopoly on militant struggles. New York City's needle trades continued to employ tens of thousands of recent immigrants: children, women, and men. In 1909 a protest meeting in the Cooper Union auditorium drew an overflow crowd of 3,000 shirtwaist workers, mostly young women. Exasperated with the appeals for caution from male union leaders, a five-foot tall, twenty-year-old worker named Clara Lemlich rose from the audience with the challenge: "I have listened to all the speakers, and I have no further patience for talk. I am one who feels and suffers from the things pictured. I move we go on a general strike!" And she led them in the Hebrew oath as her coworkers raised their right hands: "If I turn traitor to the cause I now pledge, may this hand wither from the arm I now raise." Under the banner of the Garment Workers union of the AFL, more than twenty thousand workers, the vast majority of them women, struck for higher wages and safe workplaces. Despite a small strike fund and seemingly overwhelming odds, the strikers galvanized a broad sector of labor activists, feminists, and much of the public and won significant gains.

Moderate (and mostly male) union leaders—including the AFL's Gompers—then forced a compromise settlement, over the objections of many of the most active female strikers. Not long after, some of the strikers paid a terrible price for their leaders' moderation: 146 workers died when a fire broke out in 1911 at the Triangle Shirtwaist Company, which had locked the factory doors to keep workers from "stealing" breaks or produce. Rabbi Stephen Wise thundered: "The disaster was not the deed of God but the greed of man." But one of the owners was acquitted, the other fined twenty dollars. There were massive protests, and the anger over this tragedy and injustice burned brightly among union activists for years to come. Many prominent female garment workers from this period, such as Rose Schneiderman of the International Ladies Garment Workers Union, became widely known in other reform efforts as well, including the women's suffrage movement. But her primary commitment remained the labor movement:

> The old Inquisition had its rack and its thumbscrews and its instruments of torture with iron teeth. We know what these things are today: the iron teeth are our necessities, the thumbscrews the high-powered and swift machinery close to which we must work, and the rack is here in the "fireproof" structures that will destroy us the minute they catch on fire. . . . The life of men and women is so cheap and property is so sacred. There are so many of us for one job it matters little if 143 of us are burned to death . . . I know from my experience it is up to the working people to save themselves. The only way they can save themselves is by a strong working-class movement.

Despite such passionate militancy among rank-and-file work-ers, however, many AFL union leaders saw strikes as a greater detri-ment than oppressive conditions at the workplace. Strikes bled the union treasury and sharp confrontation could generate tough employer resistance, hostile newspaper coverage, injunctions from pro-business judges—ultimately destroying unions (and union officials' jobs). A better approach, it was felt, involved cultivating better relations with more rea-sonable elements in the business community. Reaching out to prominent Progressives in the Democratic and Republican parties, AFL President Gompers also urged cooperation with "enlightened" employers who were members of the National Civic Federation.

Despite both militant and moderate strategies, substantial inequities persisted. In 1915 the richest 2 percent of the population had 50 percent of the nation's wealth, the middle 33 percent had 35 percent, and the bottom 65 percent had only 5 percent of the nation's wealth, according to U.S. government figures cited by former South Dakota Senator R. F. Pettigrew.

During World War I, which the United States entered in 1917, Gompers's strategy of cooperation seemed to pay off. The AFL sup-ported the war effort and encouraged its members not to strike while the government of Woodrow Wilson set up arbitration systems in war-time industries in which the moderate and "patriotic" union leaders were given significant influence. Membership in AFL unions increased, with about 19 percent of the nonagricultural workforce holding union cards by the war's end. By 1919 Gompers was able to comment with satisfac-tion about how the AFL majority had been able to keep "organizing and plodding along toward better conditions of life," with "its face turned toward whatever reforms, in politics or economics, could be of direct and obvious benefit to the working classes," while turning away from those who "preach and pursue that will-o'-the-wisp, a new society constructed from rainbow materials—a system of society on which even the dream-ers themselves have never agreed." The left-wing "dreamers" at whom Gompers scoffed certainly hadn't fared well during the war years.

The IWW opposed the war, as did a majority of Socialists, because they saw it as "a rich man's war and a poor man's fight" that would pit workers of various countries against each other for the benefit of their "capitalist masters." The government harassed them at every turn. In 1917, government agents arrested over 2,000 Wobblies and for the next several years, vigilante groups beat and sometimes lynched "traitorous" IWW members including war veteran Wesley Everest and the part-Cherokee Wobbly leader Frank Little. By the war's end, the entire IWW executive board were in prison, as were such outspoken Socialists as Eugene V. Debs and Kate Richards O'Hare, for violating vaguely worded "sedition" laws. The leadership of the AFL did little to protest, and some currents in the AFL gave active assistance in the government's "patriotic" repression of radicals. By 1920, thousands of left-wing workers had been jailed in the "Palmer Raids" (named after U.S. Attorney General A. Mitchell Palmer).

The repressive "red scare" was in part a reaction to recent events in Russia—a working-class revolution. "The rank and file of the Workers', Soldiers' and Peasants' Councils are in control, with Lenin and Trotsky leading," reported eyewitness journalist John Reed in the New York *Call*, the Socialist Party's daily newspaper, in November 1917. "Their program is to give the land to the peasants, to socialize natural resources and industry and for an armistice and democratic peace conference." Radicalizing workers throughout the world responded enthusiastically as V. I. Lenin and his Communist followers predicted the spread of socialist revolution to other countries. In the United States the AFL leadership around Gompers was hostile to this development, but the International Ladies Garment Workers Union spoke for other labor currents in hailing "the first truly democratic Socialist republic" and in adding that "the fate of the first great working class republic in the world cannot but be a matter of prime concern to organized and progressive workers of all countries." Naturally, such views were intolerable to U.S. business interests and governmental authorities, and they were determined to put down the threat by any means necessary.

Immigrant workers were especially targeted as a source of "un-American" influences—in some cases because they were political radicals, in some cases because they wanted unions, in some cases because they came from cultures that were different from the White Anglo-Saxon Protestant norms favored by self-styled "100 percent Americans." Some immigrants were even deported in the "red scare" hysteria. Justice was rare in the inflamed atmosphere, and two Italian American radicals, shoemaker Nicola Sacco and fish peddler Bartolomeo Vanzetti, despised in court for their anarchist opinions and their foreign accents, were convicted of robbery and murder in a blatantly unfair trial which came to symbolize the postwar antilabor repression. The case caused international working-class protests in a vain effort to stop their eventual execution.

Postwar Upsurge—and Defeat

Nonetheless, unprecedented strikes took place in 1919 and 1920. President Wilson had claimed that the World War was waged to "make the world safe for democracy," and many workers were hoping—after the wartime victory—to move forward to an expansion of democracy at home. Most surprising, perhaps, was the Boston police strike (whose crushing defeat constituted a decades-long blow to public sector unionism), but textile workers in a number of cities, coal miners in West Virginia, steelworkers from Pittsburgh to Chicago, and many others found themselves swept into a struggle for a better future and what some agitators referred to as "industrial democracy."

Like most of the big corporations, steel companies had made enormous profits from government contracts, but the steel barons refused to bargain with any union. The AFL authorized a union drive among steelworkers. This was led by onetime IWW organizer William Z. Foster, who had enjoyed some partial successes in helping Chicago's militant AFL leader John Fitzpatrick to organize packinghouse workers along industrial lines. Gompers allocated only a handful of organizers and a few thousand dollars, yet 400,000 workers, mostly immigrants, participated in the 1919 steel strike. One worker told a union rally why he risked his job: "Just like a horse and wagon, work all day. Come home— go sleep. Get up—go work in mills—come home. No know what the hell you do. For why this war? For why we buy Liberty bonds? For the mills? No, for freedom and America—for everybody. No more horse and wagon. For eight-hour day." But such "hunkies" (an ethnic slur for eastern Europeans) were beaten on the streets by mounted "Cossacks," as they called the Pennsylvania State Police, and by the steel companies' own Coal and Iron Police. Some, including union organizer Fannie Sellins, were killed. With their picket lines and meetings broken up, with many native-born workers scabbing, and with the merciless redbaiting in the press (linking the steelworkers' struggle to the Communist revolution in Russia), the strike collapsed.

One of the boldest struggles for industrial democracy took place in Seattle. The war had been unpopular, not just with the city's numerous IWW members, but also among the 25,000 AFL shipyard workers.

Throughout 1917 and 1918, first the Socialist Party and then the local AFL put out a daily labor newspaper which was critical of the war, wartime profiteering, and the vigilante justice meted out to IWWs. The paper was also supportive of the Russian Revolution and sharply critical of U.S. military attacks on the new regime there. In January 1919, a shipyard strike for higher wages quickly escalated into a general strike to protest against government indifference to working-class demands for union recognition and a decent standard of living. Workers began to reopen production (milk and coal deliveries) in order to learn to manage the economy themselves. The might of employers, the press, and the government—as well as hostility on the part of the AFL national leadership—combined to ensure the failure of the Seattle general strike.

The failure to build industrial democracy had destructive consequences. The working-class defeats of 1919 were to be felt for years to come, setting back labor's cause for decades, but the immediate effects were no less devastating. Failed strikes and crushed unions meant that returning war veterans had no legal right to their old jobs and competed for fewer and fewer jobs with the wartime workforce, which had been filled in by the northward migration of thousands of Southern black workers. Frustration and fear combined with racism and led to some of America's worst race riots in St. Louis and Chicago. There was a resurgence of the Ku Klux Klan in the North as well as the South, and the National Association for the Advancement of Colored People found that it had an uphill struggle to defend rights for African Americans throughout the country. While women had finally won the right to vote by constitutional amendment in 1920 (thanks to mounting feminist pressure in the first two decades of the twentieth century), the savage destruction of labor's strength had a chilling effect on all reform struggles, and few gains for women's rights were to be made in the new atmosphere.

Some activists in the AFL during the early 1920s were drawn to William Z. Foster's Trade Union Educational League, which like Foster became linked to the recently formed Communist Party (on its way to becoming the largest left-wing party in the country). Foster and his cothinkers were agitating for industrial unionism, a labor party, and good relations with Russia's new Soviet Republic. But Gompers and other AFL chieftains did not tolerate such a development for long, utilizing severe restrictions and large-scale expulsions against the radicals.

Somewhat more typical of the labor scene in this period was Frank Farrington of the United Mine Workers in Illinois, who "followed the Gompers philosophy of no-philosophy," as Oscar Ameringer put it, adding: "His dominating thought was always centered on the contract. He had seen too many agitators take command of a tense situation, bring the workers out onto the picket lines with fiery exhortations—and leave them there. Leave them because the rarest thing in the world is the combination of effective agitator and competent negotiator." In Ameringer's opinion, "the noblest philosophy of brotherhood, solidarity and militancy is just so much baloney if it does not finally put into the worker's hand a tightly drawn contract with his boss assuring him three square meals a day, decent working hours, and a pay envelope at the end of the week." And yet even some of the most moderate elements in the labor movement did not feel able to accept the powerful pro-business conservatism that dominated the mainstream of both the Democratic and Republican parties at this time.

In 1924 a broad array of unions (including the AFL), farmers organizations, radicals, and others sought to reverse the reactionary tide by organizing a Conference for Progressive Political Action and running the left-liberal Robert M. LaFollette for president against the Democratic and Republican candidates, advocating progressive social reforms and challenging the power of the big corporations. Although credited with a substantial 5 million votes, which might have been seen as a good beginning under other circumstances, the major forces involved were discouraged, and they subsequently abandoned this effort to push the political mainstream to the Left.

In the context of the collapsing reform efforts and rightward political drift, various forms of corruption that had existed in the labor movement for many years became dramatically more pronounced.

CHAPTER 9
Corruption

The different kinds of corruption that exist in the world can be found in the United States, among employers, in the working class, and in the labor movement. There are some who want to generalize—that the world is merely a cesspool of corruption, that the United States is simply a corrupt country, that working people are all greedy would-be crooks, that organized labor is essentially a branch of organized crime. This amounts to a grotesque distortion of reality. But the failure to acknowledge and explore the existence of corruption will also prevent us from grasping the realities of working-class history.

One form of corruption involves the growing distance between leadership and membership in many trade unions, as the leadership "machine" becomes increasingly distinct from the membership. In the 1920s, labor organizer and educator A. J. Muste described the process:

> When the [union leadership] machine first comes into power it is almost invariably because it has placed itself at the head of the mass in a great popular revolt. In such days the leaders feel themselves to be the creation of the membership and to be their servants. But gradually the leaders feel surer of their position; they get the habit of office-holding and command. They experience how ignorant and fickle and emotional the mass often is. They are less careful about consulting the membership and keeping their ear to the ground, and even if they go through all the motions of democracy as before, the mass instinctively knows that those who once felt themselves servants now regard themselves as teachers, guides, and masters; that those who once bowed down to the mass, now in their hearts despise or pity them . . .

The development of such a union organizational "machine" is often referred to as union bureaucracy—whose predominance some union

militants have castigated as "bureaucratism." In the 1960s radical labor lawyer Burton Hall wrote: "Bureaucratism is a deformity in any organization but to a labor union it can be slow (sometimes rapid) death. Seen from inside the union, it means the repression of rank-and-file opposition and the rigging of union elections; seen from outside, it involves the betrayal of union standards and the first steps toward racketeering. It has become the prime menace to unionism." Such bureaucratism became deeply ingrained in some sections of the union movement in the early years of the twentieth century.

Related to this is another form of corruption involving the shift from the social idealism, inclusiveness, and militant democracy that characterized the best of the early union movement to a narrower orientation. The development of "business unionism" concentrates on securing material privileges for an exclusive grouping of workers, instead of being concerned about the working class as a whole. The union members, more often than not, are organized not as a democratic organization but instead are under the umbrella of an autocratically run machine that collects their dues and negotiates with their employers to secure them higher wages and other benefits. This involves a transformation from being a social movement in the interest of all workers into a "special interest" that is often pitted against other workers. Labor reporter Louis Adamic put it this way:

> The attitude of the [narrow elements in the] A.F. of L. toward society at large was, in most respects, not unlike that of the capitalists. The trade-union leaders were bent upon getting for themselves and their members everything that could be had under the circumstances, whenever possible, by almost any means . . . that involved no great risks to themselves or the future of their organization. It did not concern them whether those benefits were attained at the expense of the capitalist class, the unorganized proletariat, the organized labor outside the A.F. of L., or the country as a whole. Politically, they "played the game" as it was played by the capitalists, that is, to gain immediate economic advantages and benefits. . . . They accepted the capitalist system and proposed to make the best of it.

This form of corruption contributes to the development of another form of corruption among the union leadership. "Their environment tends to make the labor leaders conservative," noted AFL insider John Frey. "When the leaders get away from the bench, their environment becomes more of the character of the employers than the workers. Moreover, the leader who rises from the rank and file at once encounters temptations hard to withstand." A higher standard of living, control over dues and strike funds, offers of "gifts" from employers, etc., leads them to "become dissipated and dishonest." Sometimes such labor leaders would collaborate with the employers against their own membership (not pushing for higher wages, etc.) or against business competitors of a particular employer (through selective strikes). "The rank and file have let their servants become their masters and dictators," complained "Mother" Mary Jones. She urged union members to fight back for control of their unions: "The workers have now to fight not alone their exploiters but likewise their own leaders, who often betray them, who sell them out, who put their own advancement ahead of that of the working masses, who make the rank and file political pawns."

A more blatant form of corruption soon developed in some sectors of the labor movement. This flowed from the utilization by some unions of violence from organized criminals in order to secure advantages that were originally supposed to come from the organized strength of their own membership and their allies in the larger working class. As Louis Adamic pointed out, criminals were first "drawn into the struggle of the haves and the have-nots" by the businessmen: "[T]hey were organized on a large scale by detective agencies and hired out, by the hundreds, as gunmen to powerful industrialists, to protect their property and scabs, and to attack strikers." Sometimes in response, "labor organizations, taking their cue from capital, began to hire professional strong-arm men to slug scabs, assassinate employers and foremen, and dynamite mills, mines, and uncompleted bridges and buildings." By the 1920s—as Harold Seidman showed in his 1938 history of labor racketeering—the gangs of professional strong-arm men "began to exert more and more influence in union affairs, and it was not long before many legitimate labor organizations . . . came under the absolute domination of the professional criminals whom they had once hired." The growing wealth and power of organized crime, gained through the lucrative bootlegging trade during the Prohibition era of the 1920s and early 1930s, made it an almost unstoppable force, particularly for union leaderships not based on strong democratic structures. (This development is a prominent theme in the 1983 gangster film *Once Upon a Time in America*, another classic film dealing with the topic from a somewhat different vantage point being *On the Waterfront*.)

In the early 1900s, racketeer Martin D. Madden ruled Chicago's Building Trades Council "by gun and blackjack," his philosophy expressed in the motto: "Show me an honest man and I'll show you a fool." But "Skinny" Madden's domination of the Chicago Federation of Labor was challenged and beaten back by progressive forces around John Fitzpatrick, who headed the city Federation for the next several decades. By the early 1930s, however, more powerful figures had muscled their way into the "labor racket," in the form of Al Capone and Frank Nitti. "When the Capone mob moved in on the milk-wagon drivers," notes Gus Tyler, "the courageous officers and members of the union fortified their headquarters and fought pitched battles with the underworld. The latter, using kidnappings, beatings, and machine guns won out."

New York City's needle trades were similarly infested with the likes of Jake Gurrah and Louis Lepke (head of the notorious "Murder Incorporated"). Union activists who combined toughness with deep-rooted idealism proved most effective in rejecting the "protective" services offered by the racketeers. Charles Zimmerman, leader of Communist dissidents in the International Ladies Garment Workers Union (before joining an ex-Communist splinter group headed by Jay Lovestone), later commented, referring to underworld strong-arm men, that "we did not need them—we had our own." Similarly, in mobilizing an eventually triumphant opposition in the corrupt Fur Workers union, popular Communist Ben Gold—after being beaten by thugs—proclaimed at a mass protest meeting: "We have decided that no more blood shall be spilled. . . . We will build a strong defense organization of the workers themselves. If it was possible to end the Czar's regime in Russia, should we be afraid of Kaufman's regime? . . . We will not stop with protest meetings. With an organized defence committee, we will take practical steps to free the workers from terror." And after a decade-long battle they finally did. By the early 1930s Sidney Hillman and Jacob Potofsky of the Amalgamated Clothing Workers were able to lead a struggle that broke the grip of what Hillman called "the racketeering evil" and "the organized blackmail system" in their union. David Dubinsky and Charles Zimmerman led an effort to push back gangster influence in the ILGWU. "Perhaps in a capitalist system built on profits and money, it is impossible to eliminate graft," Dubinsky reflected years later. "But we tried and were true to our trust." Some unions were less fortunate.

In the 1920s and 1930s, and also in later decades, anti-union employers, politicians, and propagandists focused considerable attention on union racketeering in order to generate hostility toward organized labor in general. Harold Seidman expressed the views of many honest labor activists in responding: "The cure for labor racketeering is not less unionism, but more unionism, and militant unionism." But for such genuine unionism to triumph, it would become necessary to draw away from the exclusive "what's-in-it-for-me" selfishness that had permeated so much of the labor movement. Often employers preferred narrow and corrupt unions that would be more "reasonable" than militant unions led by idealistic radicals. This resulted in many backdoor unionization efforts in which labor racketeers and employers would sign "sweetheart contracts" with little or no consultation with the workers who were being funneled into the union. This would be designed "to give the union heads an income, to give the employer relief from a real union, and to give the workers nothing," commented Gus Tyler of the ILGWU, who added: "The top men in this field are gangsters who treat unions just as another source of income, along with juke boxes, gambling, prostitution, shipping, insurance, and politics." In such a context, a corrupt union official who seemed to go out of his way to win a few gains for "his" people might even be seen as a working-class hero by some members.

Seeking to explain the attraction of organized crime for many children of the working class who were drawn into its activities (or who applauded their corrupt union leaders as "being entitled to get something for themselves since they got something for us"), sociologist Harry Elmer Barnes noted in 1934 that "both crime and racketeering today have derived their ideals and methods from the business and financial practices of the last generation," as "the younger generation looked with envy, not at the bowed backs and wrinkled brows of their parents, but rather at the financial achievements of the American financial buccaneers who made away with their millions and with little or no service to society." Endorsing this judgment, John Hutchinson, in the most comprehensive history of corruption in the U.S. labor movement, published in 1970, observed:

> The same standards conditioned the response of the business community to corruption in trade unions and labor-management relations. Extortion was usually acceptable if it meant a softening of union demands or led to a cooperative control of the market; the mistreatment of employees seldom occasioned much protest if the costs were light; the condition of business was the yardstick. Not in the building trades, nor in the garment industry, nor on the New York waterfront, nor in the service trades, nor in the entertainment industry, nor in any other seriously affected industry is there a record of substantial employer opposition to the works of the corrupt in the labor-management field. In most cases there was only collaboration or silence.

"Union corruption flourishes today because certain employers want it," Harold Seidman emphasized in the 1930s, adding: "Employers do not want an honest and virile labor movement." Neither Samuel Gompers, nor his 1925 successor William Green, nor any other top leaders of the AFL, nor a majority of AFL unions can be said to have been dominated by racketeers. Yet in C. Wright Mills's classic 1948 study of the U.S. labor movement, the important point is made that "the higher leaders of the AFL, although not engaged in the rackets themselves, have nevertheless tacitly accepted them by virtue of a do-nothing policy, because the machines upon which their jobs and powers rest have included racket-infested locals." More than this, "with its guiding philosophy [of conservatized "pure and simple" business unionism] and its expedient pragmatic course of action, the AFL has often been caught between socialist ideas on the one hand and labor-business racketeering on the other," Mills added. "In several known cases the racketeering has been given preferential support."

This development was a reflection of the serious decline of labor in the 1920s. To meet the challenges of the 1930s, however, there was the need for "an honest and virile labor movement" which would be inclusive, democratic, and socially conscious. And this would be provided to a very large extent in the great industrial union upsurge of the 1930s.

CHAPTER 10
Hardship and Resurgence

Throughout the 1920s, many unions were destroyed (in some cases through open warfare, as depicted in *Matewan*, John Sayles's powerful film about the assault on West Virginia mineworkers). Employers continued to be nervous, however, about the possibility that their workers would join the AFL, the IWW, or one of the Socialist or Communist parties. The Russian Revolution had proved popular not only in Germany, Austria, and Hungary, where workers had attempted their own revolutions, but also among energetic clusters of American workers (some influenced by the deep labor-radical subculture in the United States, others influenced by the revolutionary currents in what had been their native lands before immigrating to the United States).

Employer Triumphs
Largely in response to this undercurrent of radicalism and the more general threat of unionization, U.S. industrialists such as Henry Ford further developed innovative production and managerial techniques—begun several years earlier—to keep employees under their control. In one and the same year (1914) Ford had pioneered in (1) an assembly-line technology, the endless chain conveyor, helping to produce a standardized, low-cost automobile, and in (2) the strategy of paying dramatically higher wages than usual ($5 a day) to thwart a unionization drive by the IWW—also increasing workers' purchasing power so that they could more easily afford such consumer goods as his cars. Such innovations—called "Fordism" by some theorists—were part of the general trend by businessmen to secure their control of the workplace. The intensified wear-and-tear on his assembly-line labor force led to spectacular increases in productivity, so that by 1925 almost as many Ford autos

85

were produced in a single day as had been produced by Ford's company during the entire year of 1908. Such growth in the mass-production industries enabled employers like Ford to develop elaborate company welfare programs in the 1920s that included modest insurance and pension plans—which were designed to create employees that would conform to the company's paternalistic vision of loyalty on the job and a proper home life.

A powerful coalition of employers launched the so-called American Plan which, throughout the 1920s, successfully blocked or destroyed independent unions and secured business's far-reaching control of the workforce. On the one hand, this involved an extensive propaganda campaign against any independent labor movement as "un-American," using authoritarian methods (stool pigeons, intimidation, and repression) in the workplace to crush any efforts to organize unions. In many cases workers were forced to sign a "yellow-dog contract" promising never to join a trade union. At the same time, company-controlled grievance procedures (in some cases even company unions) were combined with paternalistic company welfare plans, "profit-sharing" schemes, and company-sponsored social activities to make employees loyal to and dependent on their benevolent bosses. Given the prosperous business climate of the 1920s, this carrot-and-stick strategy of "welfare capitalism" would prove highly effective. Union membership declined from 5 million in 1920 to 3.5 million in 1923.

Firms with welfare capitalist policies also maintained extensive spy systems, and they blacklisted "reds" and unionists. Coal camps and textile or steel towns had private police forces that maintained tight control. But even in "normal" towns and cities, employers were regularly able to get judges to issue injunctions to protect them from unions and strikes. An injunction is a legal order restraining a person or group from actions which might cause damage to someone's life or well-being or property. Union organizing efforts and strikes often were broadly interpreted as damaging the business of the employer. The outlook of many judges was expressed by the Supreme Court justice who commented that while "picketing may hardly be termed a manly occupation," there are still "some people, both men and women, [who] choose to do it and get some thrill out of it. Just why, or how, no man can say."

Louis Goldberg and Eleanore Levenson described what often occurred in the 1920s and early 1930s:

> The court issues an order forbidding picketing. [The trade union member] can no longer talk to his fellow men to persuade them to support the strike. He cannot publish in the press or through circulars that he has a grievance against the employer. He is not allowed to hold public meetings. . . . The injunction frequently goes so far as to prohibit the union from paying strike benefits and the officials from carrying on their usual duties.

More than this, it was common that "the striker in the street finds a hostile and brutal attitude on the part of the police rarely exhibited toward glamorous racketeers." This was often supplemented by the employer with his own strong-arm men, sometimes a "security" force made available from private detective agencies or other organizations specializing in strikebreaking. And a predominantly anti-union press (owned by, and largely financed with advertising from, big-business interests) sought to persuade its readers that such judges, police, and thugs were acting in the public interest.

Here and there, modest gains were made by labor activists. One of the most impressive came through the efforts of A. Philip Randolph to organize African American railroad employees (excluded from most railroad occupations that were well organized by segregated, all-white unions) into the Brotherhood of Sleeping Car Porters—but such successes were unusual in the 1920s. Randolph was a radical visionary, a veteran of the socialist movement, representing an approach not shared by most of the AFL officeholders. By the end of the decade the AFL, now led by William Green (even less combative than the late Sam Gompers), was more cautious and pessimistic than ever about the possibility—or in some cases the desirability—of organizing the masses of unskilled workers.

Related to this was another problem seriously undermining trade unionism. "In the days when the unions still possessed some militancy the conditions of organized workers always stood forth clearly as being far better than those of unorganized workers," commented William Z. Foster in a 1927 publication of the Trade Union Educational League. "But now in many cases union workers are employed under conditions little if any better than those of non-union workers. This is a deadly situation." He blamed the dominant trade-union leaders who concentrated on avoiding strikes, seeking a "higher strategy of labor" that involved cooperation with employers, and seeking to maintain a passive union membership that would not make trouble. Such labor "misleaders," he concluded, "do nothing to stir the militant spirit and class enthusiasm of the workers," even though "the great mass of workers, both organized and unorganized, live in hardship."

There was much truth in Foster's criticism. Although the 1920s are generally seen as a period of general economic prosperity—and business was certainly doing very well—it has been estimated that about 40 percent of the population lived at or below the poverty line. Things were about to get much worse.

Economic Collapse

The ten-year Great Depression hit in 1929, in part generated by the low wages of workers, who couldn't afford to buy what they made. The "welfare" paternalism of most companies collapsed, giving way to a resurgent "get-tough" policy. Troublemakers were fired or beaten up. Ford and other employers sought greater economic efficiency through the "speedup" of production. Fear stalked every worker. As the speedup intensified, forty was considered too old to work. Older workers dyed their hair in order to hold onto their jobs. By 1931, unemployment was massive. At one point, U.S. Steel didn't have a single full-time production worker—everyone was working one or two shifts a month. The company gave out baskets of food to keep its workforce off public welfare (workers who went on welfare were fired) and the costs of food baskets were deducted from workers' pay.

The devastating impact of the Depression, in human terms, is suggested when even the president of the United States asserted that one-third of the nation was ill-fed, ill-clothed, and ill-housed. It is also partly captured by photographers such as Dorothea Lange, Margaret Bourke-White, Ben Shahn, and Walker Evans (in the great tradition of Lewis Hine earlier in the century and Earl Dotter in later years). A similar imagery comes through in the classic film *Grapes of Wrath*, based on John Steinbeck's novel of the same name. Such experience had a powerful impact on working-class consciousness.

By the 1930s, labor radicals could point to forty years of failure by the mainstream unions in organizing basic industries. Auto factories, refineries, and modern steel mills were inhospitable to craft unions because most employees weren't highly skilled. Employers also made sure to hire workers who were from different countries and different races to foster divisions. Workers were afraid, and for good reason, of the company blacklist and the goon's blackjack. The harsh realities of the Great Depression seemingly made the problems faced by union organizers even greater. Organized labor had almost never included much more than 10 percent of the U.S. workforce—but in 1930 it represented less than 7 percent, about half the size of its high point ten years before. The leadership of the American Federation of Labor certainly had no hopes of organizing unorganized workers who could easily be competing with unemployed workers for a diminishing number of jobs.

Rose Pesotta, a full-time organizer for the International Ladies Garment Workers Union, complained of union officers who served as little more than "chair warmers and cigar-smokers." Finding that such union "leaders" were inclined to conduct strikes by putting a single paid picketer in front of the workplace in question, and that "rank-and-file members were not encouraged to hang around the union offices," she observed that even local union meetings were inhospitable to most workers: "The officers would take up routine matters—reading of the local's minutes, Central Labor Council minutes, the local's correspondence, then adjournment. Dull proceedings, no new faces." But the heart and soul of real trade unions, this idealistic anarchist insisted, and the only hope for a revitalized labor movement, were "a legion of men and women unheralded and unsung, rank-and-file people with natural ingenuity, strong working-class loyalty, readiness to sacrifice for an ideal, and all-around unselfishness."

Labor Upsurge

While the majority of AFL leaders had all but given up on factory workers, there were growing numbers of such workers who hadn't given up on unions. Many believed that unions, if only they might be established, could simply help them overcome on-the-job abuses and low pay, although in the face of the obvious crisis of the capitalist economy some also shared the radical sentiments of African American poet Langston Hughes:

> The bees work.
> Their work is taken from them.
> We are like the bees—
> But it won't last
> Forever.

Here and there were campaigns to rebuild unions. While most of the efforts failed, what workers learned in these struggles gave them useful experience. The IWW was largely destroyed, but here and there (as in auto) some Wobblies kept at it. Some ex-Wobblies had joined the Communist Party, which in the early 1930s had formed its own ultra-left union federation—the Trade Union Unity League—that nonetheless gave some workers organizational experience.

Socialists of various stripes joined together with some unions to form the Brookwood Labor College in New York State, headed by radical minister A. J. Muste, which trained working-class activists in the basics of history, economics, sociology, writing skills, and basic organizing techniques. As James Maurer, a longtime leader of the Pennsylvania Federation of Labor, Socialist, and Brookwood supporter, noted: "My lifelong association with working people in the city and on the farm, skilled and unskilled, organized and unorganized, has taught me that their greatest weakness is lack of knowledge concerning their existence, and this long ago turned my thoughts to workers' education." In addition to Brookwood, labor-supported institutions that tried to rectify this situation included Work People's College in Minnesota, Commonwealth College in Arkansas, Highlander Folk School in Tennessee, and the Bryn-Mawr Summer School for Women Workers. Labor education was also carried on by education departments in a few unions (such as the International Ladies Garment Workers Union and the Amalgamated Clothing Workers of America), by the Communist and Socialist parties (for example, in New York City's Workers School and Rand School, respectively), as well as by the far more moderate Wisconsin School for Workers affiliated with the University of Wisconsin (and influenced by such scholarly advocates of "pure and simple" unionism as Selig Perlman).

There were also Unemployed Councils, Unemployed Leagues, and locals of the Workers Alliance mobilizing those who were out-of-work to struggle for government assistance, housing for the unemployed, etc. These and other efforts as labor journalist Art Preis later noted, "trained hundreds of thousands of workers in labor organization and class-struggle tactics." This helped prepare the groundwork for a new upsurge in basic industry that would change the face of the labor movement and of U.S. society as a whole.

By the early 1930s, militancy was on the rise. In 1934, there were signs that workers could win if they had capable leaders. In Minneapolis, Vincent Raymond Dunne and other dissident-Communist followers of Leon Trotsky (who opposed the Stalin dictatorship that had taken over in the decade following the Russian Revolution) led thousands of teamsters and others to victory through a militant general strike that used bold new tactics such as roving pickets utilizing automobiles and directed via radio. In San Francisco, mainstream Communists allied with Harry Bridges led West Coast longshoremen to a partial victory after a hard-fought general strike. In Ohio, Toledo Auto-Lite workers, led by A. J. Muste and his socialist followers in the American Workers Party, won a similar victory. Big membership gains were also made through organizing efforts by mineworkers, garment workers, and clothing workers.

There were also some painful defeats. Without effective leadership and organization, workers' militancy failed to build unions. The United Textile Workers—with minimal strike funds and an overly optimistic expectation of support from the reform-minded administration of the newly elected President Franklin D. Roosevelt—called a nation-wide strike, with especially large numbers of union members in the Southern states. (The Democratic President was not inclined to alienate the anti-union and racist political forces in that region—the so-called Dixiecrats—that were an important component of his own party.) One Southern employer had commented: "I don't care if any of my workers join a union—just so they don't tell me about it." Employers saw the strike as a war in which they mobilized far more resources than the union was able to employ: martial law, the National Guard, goon squads and gun thugs, Pinkerton spies, as well as antiunion newspapers and radio stations. Sixteen workers were killed and many more were wounded, the strike was crushed, and 15,000 strikers were blacklisted. The cause of labor in the South was set back for many years to come.

Yet the balance of power in the labor struggles of 1934 had tilted decisively in labor's favor. And the leaders of the victorious labor insurgencies tended to be deeply rooted in their communities, with strong ties to their coworkers, and at the same time animated by fiercely radical ideas. "Our policy was to organize and build strong unions so workers could have something to say about their own lives and assist in changing the present order into a socialist society," V. R. Dunne matter-of-factly explained of his efforts in leading workers of his hometown to victory. "Probably four or five hundred workers in Minneapolis knew 'Ray' personally," journalist Charles Walker later commented. "They formed their own opinions—that he was honest, intelligent, and selfless, and a damn good organizer for the truck drivers' union to have. They had always known him to be a Red; that was no news." On the West Coast, Harry Bridges, leader of the radicalized International Longshore and Warehouseman's Union, did not hesitate in expressing the opinion that "the capitalistic form of society . . . means the exploitation of a lot of people for a profit and a complete disregard of their interests for that profit, [and] I haven't much use for that." Many of his members saw things the same way. The established labor leadership felt new pressures and a new vulnerability from below.

CIO and Labor Radicalism

The rapid rise of left-led unions, mass strikes, and rank-and-file workers' movements inspired workers throughout the country, and also generated ferment within the AFL. John L. Lewis of the United Mine Workers,

David Dubinsky of the International Ladies Garment Workers Union, Sidney Hillman of the Amalgamated Clothing Workers of America, Charles Howard of the International Typographical Union, and others urged the Federation to launch an organizing drive among the country's mass-production workers, and to form unions along industrial rather than craft lines. In 1935 they formed a Committee for Industrial Organization within the AFL, which resulted in their expulsion from the AFL by late 1936. Despite bitter AFL denunciations of them as apostles of "dual unionism" (with which the IWW had been tagged in earlier years), CIO organizers and activists continued to surge forward throughout 1937, and in the following year they formally established the Congress of Industrial Organizations. Lewis emphasized the existence—currently outside the ranks of organized labor—of "a great reservoir of workers here numbering millions and millions of men and women, and back of them stand great numbers of millions of dependents," who wanted "a policy that will permit them to join with us in this great fight for the maintenance of the rights of workers and for the upholding of the standards of modem democracy."

The trademark of the CIO seemed to be the stern visage and militant, biblical oratory of John L. Lewis. His reputation in the labor movement for conservatism and running a top-down union regime were balanced by his clear understanding that workers were ready to organize and that new tactics were needed. The scourge of labor radicals within his own union for decades, he proved quite willing to work closely with many whom he had bitterly fought in earlier years. Such was the case with John Brophy, expelled from the UMW for opposing Lewis with a left-wing "Save the Union" movement in the 1920s but taken back into the UMW in the early 1930s and appointed CIO director of organization in 1935. Lewis's own powerful rhetoric tilted leftward in the new situation.

Blaming the Depression and the decline of workers' quality of life on industrial policies "determined by a small, inner group of New York bankers and financiers," Lewis emphasized that "organized labor has determined that this sinister financial and industrial dictatorship must be destroyed." This was to be accomplished through the efforts of inclusive new industrial unions that would establish "genuine collective bargaining" with the big corporations, and also through political organization "by the labor groups, whether hand or brain workers, to the end that it may be used in cooperation with other unselfish groups of our people in establishing sound measures of industrial democracy, and in bringing about other social, economic, and humanitarian reforms which are traditionally and indissolubly associated with the ideals and aspirations of our self-governing republic."

In early 1936 rubber workers seized control of the Goodyear plant in Akron, Ohio with a sit-down strike and quick victory that established the United Rubber Workers of America as the first CIO success story. CIO resources and staff moved in to assist local Socialists and Trotskyists "who had been at the hub of Akron's organizing campaigns," as the noted labor writer Sidney Lens later commented. Communists and other radicals were in the forefront of the tough-fought union victories in the summer and fall of 1936 over General Electric and the Radio Corporation of America (RCA) that put the United Electrical, Radio and Machine Workers of America on the map as another CIO triumph.

In the auto industry, too, the CIO succeeded because of a rank-and-file upsurge. In Flint, Michigan, workers staged a sit-down strike that lasted several weeks and shut down much of General Motors Corporation's production—resulting in a resounding victory for the newly formed United Automobile Workers of America. U.S. Steel sought to avoid such turmoil and signed a national agreement with the CIO's Steel Workers Organizing Committee even though the union's base among steelworkers was relatively weak. Another large company, Jones and Laughlin, agreed to a union election after a brief strike. In order to enforce contracts, the early CIO relied on workers' own solidarity. Shop stewards collected dues directly from workers, and union leaders had to address grievances immediately. Workers resolved shopfloor problems by engaging in short "quickie" strikes or slow downs. On an assembly line or in a modern mill or refinery, even a small group of workers could cripple production. Just as the Wobblies had preached, these tactics inflicted maximum pain on employers with minimum risk to workers. The UAW rank-and-file also showed a preference for tough and experienced organizers with left-wing backgrounds, such as Walter, Victor, and Roy Reuther; Wyndham Mortimer; Robert Travis; Emil Mazey; and a host of energetic activists.

Among these were Genora Johnson Dollinger and others who organized the colorful "Women's Emergency Brigade" (depicted in the stirring documentary film *With Babies and Banners*) that played a key role in winning the Flint strike. The Brigade evolved out of the UAW's Women's Auxiliary. "The core group decided that whereas all of the other AFL auxiliaries were called Ladies Auxiliaries and they had their box socials and little parties and things like that, but didn't really know anything about labor or conditions in the country," Dollinger later recalled, "we decided we were *women* and we didn't want any of this *lady* stuff, so we called ourselves for the first time in the American labor movement the Women's Auxiliary of the UAW." Although some of the union men "remained just as chauvinistic as ever," others "who were really union men and were much more open to having the forces to build a union and win a strike were very grateful and told us many times how happy they were in their homes since their wives got active." The women who were involved "were changing almost day by day . . . standing a little taller and talking to the men a little more sure of themselves." Such female militants inspired radical songwriter Woody Guthrie—part of a group of radical union troubadours known as The Almanac Singers—to write the famous song "Union Maid":

> There once was a union maid who never was afraid
> of goons and ginks and company finks
> And the deputy sheriffs who made the raid;
> She went to the union hall when a meeting it was called,
> And when the company boys came 'round
> She always stood her ground.
> Oh, you can't scare me, I'm sticking to the union.
> I'm sticking to the union, I'm sticking to the union.
> Oh, you can't scare me, I'm sticking to the union.
> I'm sticking to the union till the day I die.*

Such changing attitudes were largely a result of radicals' efforts. Dollinger was herself a member of the Socialist Party at that time (and later a Trotskyist). In an interview in the 1990s, she still emphasized the importance of left-wing influence in helping build a consciousness vital for strengthening the union struggles:

It happened that the headquarters for the Socialist Party, the Proletarian Party, and the Socialist Labor Party were all in the same big historic building where the union offices were on one floor. It was an old, rickety building but it was something we could afford. And workers were coming

---

* UNION MAID. Words and Music by Woody Guthrie TRO-©-Copyright 1961 (Renewed) 1963 (Renewed) Ludlow Music, Inc., New York, New York. Used by permission.

up to find out what could be done and we would get to know them. We gave classes in labor history to let them know that there were gains that had been made and that there were labor leaders who had given their lives for the organization of labor.

Although many of the new CIO officers and members could hardly be considered political radicals, in a number of the new unions, various Socialists, Communists, and Trotskyists assumed key roles as selfless organizers and respected leaders.

The radical fervor also found reflection in its understanding of the necessity to overcome racial divisions. The new labor federation asserted that "the CIO pledges itself to uncompromising opposition to any form of discrimination, whether political or economic, based on race, color, creed, or nationality." While shortcomings could certainly be found in how this sentiment was implemented, the country's leading African American newspaper, the *Pittsburgh Courier*, remarked that "the only real effort that has been made to let down the color bars since the days of the Knights of Labor is that of the Congress of Industrial Organizations." The NAACP's chief legal advisor, Thurgood Marshall, concurred: "The program of the CIO has become a Bill of Rights for Negro labor in America."

Editor of the *CIO News* Len DeCaux has described the early CIO as not simply a new labor federation but as "a mass movement with a message, revivalistic in fervor, militant in mood, joined together by class solidarity." On Labor Day 1937, CIO chieftain John L. Lewis, in order to express the CIO message, intoned: "This movement of labor will go on until there is a more equitable and just distribution of our national wealth. This movement will go on until the social order is reconstructed on a basis that will be fair, decent, and honest. This movement will go on until the guarantees of the Declaration of Independence and of the Constitution are enjoyed by all the people, and not by a privileged few." Writing in 1938, labor journalist Mary Heaton Vorse commented: "Labor has shown in its struggles an inventiveness, intelligence, and power greater than anything before in its long history. Whole communities of workers have been transformed." Looking back on this period, DeCaux elaborated:

> As it gained momentum, this movement brought with it new political attitudes—toward the corporations, toward police and troops, toward

local, state, national government. Now we're a movement, many workers asked, why can't we move on to more and more? Today we've forced almighty General Motors to terms by sitting down and defying all the powers at its command, why can't we go on tomorrow, with our numbers, our solidarity, our determination, to transform city and state, the Washington government itself? Why can't we go on to create a new society with the workers on top, to end age-old injustices, to banish poverty and war.

The New Deal

The labor upsurge and radicalization created a remarkable change in the country's political climate. In 1932, the Norris-LaGuardia Act had already outlawed the "yellow-dog contract" and deprived federal courts of the power to issue the sweeping anti-union injunctions (against union activity, strikes, picketing, etc.) that had been so common in previous decades. In the same year, Democratic Presidential candidate Franklin D. Roosevelt had been swept into office promising Depression-ridden America a "New Deal." The first term of his administration seemed to balance pro-business and pro-labor policies in a somewhat dubious National Recovery Act which was declared unconstitutional but which (while it lasted) gave workers the right to organize unions by federal law. By 1936, under the impact of the early CIO gains and radical working-class pressure, Roosevelt's New Deal tilted in a much more pro-labor direction. The President denounced as "economic royalists" those conservative businessmen who vociferously objected to his programs—while at the same time explaining that he was doing all this to save capitalism, which some of the more sophisticated corporate executives understood quite clearly.

Nonetheless, the sweeping package of New Deal social reforms went far beyond any government programs even of the pre–World War I Progressive era—creating Social Security, public works projects, unemployment insurance, and much more that was beneficial to U.S. working people. One of the most far-reaching pieces of legislation was the National Labor Relations Act of 1935, commonly known as the Wagner Act, which established the collective bargaining framework that defines today's labor unions. In sharp contrast to the past, unions no longer built organizations that negotiated with employers based on the sheer strength of skill or solidarity, but could rely on government-monitored elections (through the National Labor Relations Board) to win recognition. Workplace grievances didn't have to result in strikes, but could be arbitrated through a special court system, and rulings had the force of law.

Some analysts have argued that unions' reliance on the government's labor-relations system played a major role in undermining labor's radicalism and independence. Union leaderships were, more often than not, inclined to rely on the lengthy arbitration process rather than the often quicker and more decisive resort to local strike action. Government regulations were designed to thwart rank-and-file militancy, and unions found that attempts to buck the new labor relations system could result in the loss of the very real protections and advantages provided by the NLRB and other aspects of the Wagner Act. Once contracts were signed, union officials were generally expected to enforce the contract with their members—accepting the employer's authority at the workplace, preventing "wildcat" and "quickie" strikes, enforcing discipline. The fact remained that immense gains were made by organized labor under the Wagner Act.

The ranks of the CIO were swelled by new industrial unions in steel, electrical, auto, longshore, maritime, transit, rubber, textile, and more. Soon the AFL moved in a similar direction to maintain its own survival. Some AFL unions, such as the International Brotherhood of Teamsters, were transformed from craft organizations into mass-industrial unions (in this case thanks to the influence of the Minneapolis Trotskyists—the Dunne brothers, Carl Skoglund, Farrell Dobbs, and others) with considerable idealism and enthusiastic response from a broad range of workers. The AFL's Amalgamated Meatcutters and Butcher Workmen led by Socialist Pat Gorman also embraced industrial unionism, reaching out to workers of many trades.

But certain other growth-conscious AFL unions concentrated on "organizing the employers" rather than organizing the workers. A. O. Wharton, the anti-leftist (and anti-Semitic) president of the AFL International Association of Machinists, sent out a letter to his staff in 1937 indicating that many employers would strongly prefer to deal with a conservative AFL organization than with the radical-tainted CIO. "Since the Supreme Court decision upholding the Wagner Labor Act, many employers now realize that it is the Law of our Country and they are prepared to deal with labor organizations," Wharton wrote.

"These employers have expressed a preference to deal with AFL organizations rather than Lewis, Hillman, Dubinsky, Howard and that gang of sluggers, communists, radicals and soapbox artists, professional bums, expelled members of labor unions, outright scabs and the Jewish organizations with all their red affiliates."* Sidney Lens has commented that in the late 1930s and 1940s "hundreds of thousands of workers were dragooned into the AFL; many, if not most, without being consulted and against their will." Nonetheless, the rivalry with the CIO often forced AFL organizations to push for improved wages and working conditions, and the swelling of labor's ranks was changing the balance of power within the United States.

Another significant force—influenced by the anarchist-pacifist Catholic Worker movement of Dorothy Day—emerged within "the rough-and-tumble world," as historian Mel Piehl put it, "where unreconstructed employers, union toughs, Communists, gangsters, and labor priests waged battle for the allegiance of workers." This was the Association of Catholic Trade Unionists (ACTU), which enthusiastically threw itself into helping to build the industrial unions of the CIO, believing that "side by side with these unions must be Catholic associations which aim at giving their members moral and religious training." An aspect of the ACTU's ideology was expressed by one of its architects, John Cort, who envisioned a future when "workers who are capable of creative effort once again become 'workers' in the true sense, and no longer the unthinking slaves of machinery and stockholders. Then industrial democracy will reign not only in each plant and company, but throughout the national economy." Industrial unionism

---

* Ironically, half a century later, the president of the International Association of Machinists would articulate precisely the orientation that IAM President Wharton was attacking. "You don't have to be a Marxist to observe the conflict between labor and capital is as old as the history of the world," wrote IAM President William Winpisinger in the 1980s. "Each one's behavior has been remarkably consistent throughout history. Labor always seeks to preserve and improve its material lot, to gain a greater share of the wealth it produces, and to achieve a greater degree of economic and political freedom. Capital is remarkably consistent in its resistance to labor's quest. Corporate management has always relied on absolute power, authority and control—the ultimate and most ancient order of political supremacy—to achieve its goals of cost minimization, market domination and profit maximization.... When labor is militant, history tells us, trade union goals are advanced...."

could lead the way against "greed and profiteering" toward guarantee-ing "a living wage" for all, eventually—as Piehl put it—creating a future when "capitalism might be gradually transformed into the humane and Christian economic order envisioned by the popes" in their encyclicals *Rerum Novarum* (1891) and *Quadragesimmo Anno* (1931). Through the efforts of activists such as Cort, Martin Wesing, Father Charles Owen Rice, and others, the ACTU helped organize unions, win strikes, push back gangsterism—and also to develop an alternative to Marxist ideas and to challenge the influence of the Communist Party. According to historian of U.S. anti-Communism John Haynes: "Hundreds of workers who had passed through the ACTU's training sessions in parliamentary procedure, organizing, labor law, bookkeeping, and, of course, Catholic social philosophy and anticommunism, became officials of union locals."

In 1937 the CIO had 1.5 million members, while the AFL had about 2.5 million; by 1941 the size of both labor federations had almost dou-bled—and close to one-third of the workforce was unionized. In the Southern states of the former Confederacy, however, where conservative racist regimes had assumed power in the post-Reconstruction era fol-lowing 1877, the continuing repressive political climate combined with sharp racial divisions within the working class to limit or block the stun-ning labor victories that swept much of the North and the West. Extreme violence, intimidation, race-baiting, and red-baiting were utilized to smash the efforts of Southern textile workers and others to advance the union cause. Yet enough gains were made by CIO organizers elsewhere to convince many that it would only be a matter of time before the South went the way of the rest of the country.

In contrast to the situation in most industrialized countries, however, the labor movement did not have its own political party. Instead, for the most part, unions in the United States were integrated into the New Deal alliance of the Democratic Party under President Franklin D. Roosevelt (known by his initials "FDR")—which included many of the conserva-tive Southern politicians who opposed union organizing in their home states. A related problem was that FDR's primary commitment was not to his working-class supporters—he was no less committed to the inter-ests of big business, which sometimes meant giving labor the short end of the stick. And by the late 1930s, when he was beginning to shift the country to a war footing in preparation for the fast-approaching Second

World War, he proved more than willing to jettison many of the New Deal social reforms.

As the newly organized unions solidified at the end of the Depression decade, it became clear that far from destroying capitalism, as many employers had feared, the government's support for unions had stabilized capitalism. FDR's balancing act was highlighted in 1937 when strikers at Republic Steel were shot in the back in the Memorial Day Massacre: the President employed the phrase "a plague on both your houses," equating union victims with the police and the steel thugs who had victimized them. While FDR's Democratic Party relied on workers' votes and unions' organizational muscle, the party never wavered in its support for the "liberty" of corporations and the free-market system. This highlights a difference between the U.S. labor movement and those in Europe, insightfully summarized by historian Lizabeth Cohen:

> In Europe, where workers were more anti-capitalist, they supported unions and political parties that demanded more radical changes, helping in some cases . . . to establish welfare states that were more Socialist in orientation, and in others . . . to make workers less integrated into mainstream political parties. American workers, in contrast, even when they harbored a "class" agenda as in the 1930s, turned to an existing mainstream political institution like the Democratic Party to achieve it. As a result, although at the time many individual workers and CIO officials hoped to accomplish working-class objectives through the Democratic Party, the reality of the party's broad base early on committed it to multiple, and ultimately less progressive, goals.

CIO President John L. Lewis—whose strong personality increasingly clashed with that of Roosevelt—had helped to establish the firm labor-Democratic alliance of the 1930s, but by the end of the decade had come to distrust it, expressing the view that organized labor must preserve a certain amount of political independence. Roosevelt's "plague on both your houses" comment drew this widely quoted rebuke from the union chieftain: "Labor, like Israel, has many sorrows. Its women weep for their fallen, and they lament for the future of the children of the race. It ill behooves one who has supped at labor's table and who has been sheltered in labor's house to curse with equal fervor and fine impartiality both labor and its adversaries when they become locked in deadly embrace." When Roosevelt announced that he would run for a third term in 1940, Lewis argued that the CIO should not support him.

Some thought the CIO leader might call for the formation of a new labor party—but instead he took the more "pragmatic" stand of backing the liberal Republican candidate, Wendell Wilkie. When the bulk of the CIO did not follow this course, Lewis resigned as president of the CIO. As Roosevelt swept on to a third presidential victory, the nation's economy was coming out of the Great Depression—not because of the New Deal policies, but because the approaching Second World War (which had already begun in Europe and Asia) was good for U.S. business, which was revitalized by war production.

A new era was about to dawn.

CHAPTER 11

The Second World War and Its Aftermath

Sometimes World War II is seen by Americans as "the good war," a crusade against the brutal militaristic expansionism, the murderous racism, the vicious dictatorships of the Axis powers; a worldwide "people's war" against the Nazi, fascist, and imperial regimes dominating Germany, Italy, and Japan and seeking to subjugate the entire world. Many saw the war against the Axis powers as a struggle for a postwar world in which all could enjoy the "the Four Freedoms"—freedom of expression, freedom of thought and religion, freedom from fear, freedom from want. Some in the U.S. labor movement of 1940 believed (with John L. Lewis) that in some ways it was also a power struggle—including a struggle for markets, raw materials, and economic conquest, similar to what World War I had turned out to be—that would destroy the lives of millions of innocent people. But by the time of the 1941 attack on Pearl Harbor, which brought the United States into the war as an official combatant, the bulk of the AFL and CIO were prepared to give thoroughgoing support to the U.S. war effort.

Many workers joined the armed forces, and many more were drafted. On the homefront, millions of workers flooded into the now-booming war industries generated or regenerated by generous government contracts. Millions of women and African Americans were drawn into what, for them, had been "nontraditional jobs," and the booming industries yielded spectacular profits for big-business corporations (as well as smaller profiteers) while churning out massive quantities of war materiel essential to the victory of the wartime alliance—the United States,

Britain, France, the Soviet Union, China, and many other nations—over the Axis powers.

Home Front

The CIO's new president, soft-spoken Philip Murray (who earlier had moved from the United Mine Workers to head the new Steelworkers union), and his AFL counterpart, William Green, promised organized labor's adherence to wage and price controls and a no-strike pledge for the duration of the war. A War Labor Board was established to oversee and negotiate industrial relations, with substantial union representation, which—among other things—oversaw (with the National Labor Relations Board) the unionization of hundreds of thousands of new wartime workers, a bitter pill for employers that was thickly sugar-coated with soaring wartime profits and guarantees that the unions would help enforce industrial discipline and the no-strike pledge.

Amalgamated Clothing Workers president Sidney Hillman was made associate director of the Office of Production Management, tirelessly seeking to maintain workers' discipline on the job while at the same time defending the interests of labor in the wartime economy. He urged Roosevelt to adopt an expansive wartime program of economic, social, and labor reform that would involve taxation falling most heavily on the rich, a stricter policy of price controls, the equitable rationing of basic commodities, union security, and "equality of sacrifice"—but he was snubbed and demoted for his pains. Leading up to the 1944 elections, Hillman was able to mobilize enough labor pressure to force the President to give lip service to an Economic Bill of Rights "guaranteeing" full employment at decent wages, aid to farmers, government regulation of industry, cradle-to-grave social security, and decent housing, health care, and education to all as a matter of right. This far-reaching vision of social justice was never enacted, however, and the pro-labor political rhetoric was more than offset by pro-business economic policies.

John L. Lewis and the United Mine Workers—angry over war profiteering at the expense of workers' needs and dignity—challenged the no-strike pledge in a series of 1943 coal strikes. In the previous year, after Lewis's unsuccessful effort to engineer AFL-CIO unity in order to more effectively withstand government and employer pressures, the UMW had left the CIO (briefly rejoining the AFL in 1946). Both labor federations denounced Lewis's militant wartime tactics. But the miners' action was emulated by thousands of rank-and-file workers in other industries who conducted an unprecedented wave of "wildcat" strikes over a number of shopfloor grievances in 1944 and 1945.

Those who went "too far," however, risked heavy persecution. Trotskyists leading the powerful Minneapolis Teamsters were critical of the war aims of the U.S. government, which they said were geared to advance the domestic and overseas interests of U.S. corporations, and to which they counterposed a socialist working-class program for defeating fascism. Government prosecutions led to the imprisonment of James P. Cannon, V. R. Dunne, and sixteen other revolutionary socialists under the newly passed Smith Act.* While many unions protested this political persecution and violation of free speech, few protested an even more extreme injustice: hundreds of thousands of innocent Japanese Americans were deprived of their jobs and homes and herded into detention camps for the duration of the war simply because of their race and national origin.

Equal Rights

On the other hand, significant gains were made against prejudice in other sectors of the home front. At the early stages of the war, companies had continued their long-standing racist hiring practices (which was

---

* This repression was carried out with the full support of conservative and bureaucratic elements in the International Brotherhood of Teamsters. Breaking the left-wing influence facilitated the expansion of gangster-linked elements in the union.

reflected in the U.S. military, whose units remained racially segregated throughout the Second World War). Yet with the United States preparing to be involved in a war against Nazi efforts to establish the supremacy of a "master race" in Europe, the U.S. government was vulnerable to a threatened march on Washington for racial equality by thousands of black workers led by A. Philip Randolph of the Brotherhood of Sleeping Car Porters. In exchange for the calling off of the march, Roosevelt signed an executive order pledging to protect the rights of black and female workers in companies with wartime contracts. Through the Fair Employment Practices Commission, black and female unionists had a potent weapon to challenge companies, and hundreds of thousands of workers ultimately benefited. Union halls from Detroit to Birmingham were the center of the civil rights movement as radical whites and blacks fought racism on the job and segregation in the community.

Many of the new women workers did not participate in the union. "The women felt the union was a man's thing because once they got through the day's work they had another job," union activist Stella Nowicki recalled. "When they got home they had to take care of their one to fifteen children and the meals and the house and all the rest, and the men went to the tavern and to the [union] meetings and to the racetrack and so forth." Struggling to overcome this sexism, and sometimes helping to make genuine gains (such as child-care facilities at the workplace and increased women's involvement in the union), Nowicki continued to be frustrated by insufficient union concern over the needs of its female members: "The unions had so many things they had to work for—the shorter work day, improved conditions—so many things that they couldn't worry about these things in relation to women."

Postwar Triumphs

With the end of the war in 1945, the FEPC was dismantled, and government protection of minority workers ended. Most women workers were fired. Some protested, like the women Ford workers who pointed out that "the hand that rocks the cradle can build tractors too." Although black men were not exactly told to make room for returning white veterans, the best seniority could do was to uphold the policy of last hired, first fired. At worst, seniority could be used to hold black workers into separate job lines or "Negro" departments. Racial segregation, discrimination, and prejudice persisted—in the Southern states maintained most systematically with the force of law, violence, and lynching. (On the other hand, returning black veterans—most of whom were part of the working class—were less inclined than ever to accept racism at home after helping to defeat it abroad: the stage was set for the rise of the modem civil rights movement.)

With the end of World War II, many unionists expected employers to counterattack and attempt to destroy the unions as they did after World War I. There were also fears that—with the end of wartime stimulus— another economic depression would devastate the country. But reality unfolded differently.

As labor journalist Art Preis commented, 1945–1946 saw "American labor's greatest upsurge," with a massive eruption of postwar strikes— mobilizing 3,470,000 workers in 1945 and 4,600,000 in 1946, in each case far exceeding the number of strikers of 1937, the most tumultuous year of the Depression decade. The militant strikers enjoyed widespread community support, and far from being crushed (as had been the case in 1919) they were overwhelmingly victorious. Auto, steel, electrical, rubber, and other workers successfully raised wages in line with business's high prices and profits. In addition, regarding the organization of unions throughout the South as a key to the long-run success of the labor movement, the CIO with great fanfare announced "Operation Dixie"—a plan to mobilize the entire labor movement to aid in unionizing the South. It seemed that the dynamic industrial unions were here to stay, and the consequence was the beginning of a steady rise in the living standards— and buying power—of U.S. workers for the next twenty-five years, which would help fuel general economic prosperity. Many of the New Deal social programs remained in place, and Roosevelt's Democratic successor, Harry Truman, promised a continuation of such policies with his "Fair Deal."

There were efforts to alter the economy in even more fundamental ways. In 1946, the United Auto Workers, under pressure from its left wing, challenged General Motors to "open the books" to prove that workers could receive a raise without a rise in prices, and union negotiator Walter Reuther explicitly put forward the highly publicized demand that a raise in auto workers' pay not be passed on to the consumer. The union won its raise, but union leaders subsequently avoided such radical challenges to "management's right to manage." In 1948, however, the

UAW did secure the first cost-of-living escalator clause, so that at least some union members' pay increases would keep pace with rising prices.

In the wake of the 1946 strikes labor-relations scholar Sumner H. Slichter suggested that postwar America might be "gradually shifting from a capitalistic economy to a laboristic one—that is to a community in which employees rather than businessmen are the strongest single influence." The only way such an outcome could be prevented would be—in the words of historian Elizabeth Fones-Wolf—if "important segments of the business community responded to this economic and ideological challenge with an aggressive campaign . . . to undermine the legitimacy and power of organized labor."

CHAPTER 12

Cold War and Social Compact

U.S. corporations *did* launch a counterattack against what they insisted was excessive union power and against radical labor challenges to "America's free enterprise system." Massively financed pro-business propaganda campaigns dovetailed with big contributions to the election campaigns of pro-business Republicans and Democrats—culminating in conservative congressional amendments to the nation's labor law. The Taft-Hartley Act of 1947 did not outlaw unions outright—public opinion and working-class power would no longer permit that—but rather was designed to moderate and de-radicalize the labor movement. Limitations on picketing, prohibition of secondary strikes and boycotts, the imposition of "cooling-off periods," and other governmental controls were designed to undercut the natural militancy and organizing techniques that had been so effective in the 1930s and again in 1946.* There was also a ban on direct union contributions to political parties (there were no such restrictions on businesses)—in part to undercut labor support to the Democratic Party, but perhaps in part to hinder the future development of the sort of union-based Labor Party that had recently swept into office in Britain. Another key provision of the Taft-Hartley Act was that union officers could not be members of the Communist Party, and that all labor officials must sign non-Communist affidavits if their organizations were to be granted labor-law protections.

---

* "The 'cooling-off' provisions are in the Act not for the purpose of making labor think twice and encouraging it to find a solution without resorting to a strike," left-wing labor analyst John Steuben observed. Rather the Taft-Hartley 60-day "cooling-off period" means that, in addition to eliminating the often important element of surprise from strike strategy, "a status quo condition is established for the union while the employers gather every conceivable weapon for use against the proposed strike."

John L. Lewis was one of the few non-Communist union leaders who called for militant action to oppose this and other Taft-Hartley provisions that would "make more difficult the securing of new members for this labor movement, without which our movement will become so possessed of inertia that there is no action and no growth." Denouncing the act as "bought and paid for by campaign contributions from the industrial and business interests of this country," he warned the 1947 convention of the AFL: "If you resist the power of the state, the central government will be used against you, and if you don't resist it will be used against you that much more quickly, because they won't lose any sleep at night worrying about what to do with a labor movement that is fleeing before the storm." When the AFL leadership rejected this militant approach (one of its rising stars from the Plumber's union, George Meany, red-baited Lewis's record as former head of the CIO), the UMW pulled out of the AFL and remained for years in lofty isolation from both labor federations which had accommodated themselves to the new status quo. (Several years later, Meany himself confessed that union organizing efforts were not nearly as successful as they used to be because, by utilizing the Taft-Hartley Act, "any employer who wants to resist organization and is willing to make his plant a battleground for that resistance can very effectively prevent organization of his employees.")

Communism and Anti-Communism

The anti-Communist provision of Taft-Hartley—designed to amputate labor's left wing and intimidate those influenced by radical ideas—was closely related to postwar international developments. The United States had emerged from World War II as the foremost economic, political, and military power on earth, and many business and political leaders confidently predicted that the next hundred years would constitute "the American Century." On the other hand, they were concerned that the experiences of World War II and popular postwar aspirations would generate revolutions sweeping radical, left-wing, and in some cases Communist regimes into power. This would tear much of the international economy out of the capitalist orbit, with negative consequences for U.S. businesses. Soon a global confrontation crystallized—labeled the "cold war"—between pro-U.S. and pro-capitalist regimes vs. the Soviet Union and countries in Eastern Europe and Asia where Communist regimes had come to power.

In a variety of countries there were many workers and intellectuals, peasants and oppressed people who had high hopes that the Communist movement arising out of the 1917 workers' revolution in Russia—led by V. I. Lenin and other left-wing Marxists—could lead to a new era of freedom, prosperity, and dignity for all. But the early revolutionary socialist idealism of that movement became increasingly offset by the brutal bureaucratic dictatorship that had crystallized in Russia during the 1920s and 1930s.* Nor were independent trade unions, freedom of expression, or genuinely democratic elections tolerated in the new Communist countries of the late 1940s—facts that were known by many union members in the United States and elsewhere. The Communist dictatorships claimed to be implementing "socialism," which eventually tainted that term in the minds of millions.

The U.S. government and business community widely criticized such grim realities in massive anti-Communist propaganda campaigns, which were at the same time aggressive public relations efforts for an interpretation of "the American way of life" that emphasized the centrality of corporate capitalism. In its defense of "freedom," however, U.S. foreign

---

* This degeneration began during the brutal civil war period of 1918–1921 but was consolidated with the ascendancy of a bureaucratic elite of the Russian Communist Party, headed by the ruthless personality of Josef Stalin, which came into its own after Lenin's death in 1924, and with the defeat of Trotsky's Left Opposition in 1927 and of moderate elements around Nikolai Bukharin in 1929. The consolidation of what some referred to as "Stalinism" resulted in repression and death in the Soviet Union for millions of peasants, workers, and intellectuals (including many who believed in the original high ideals of Communism), as well as the erosion of the revolutionary-democratic qualities of Communist Parties throughout the world.

policy warmly embraced and defended unpopular anti-Communist dictatorships in capitalist countries that were friendly to U.S. businesses.

The defense of the corporations' economic interests abroad was certainly vital to the health of the U.S. business economy. The confrontation with the Soviet Union also generated an arms race and massive military spending that acted as a tremendous economic stimulus. By the late 1950s, Republican President Dwight D. Eisenhower felt compelled to warn about the resulting "military-industrial complex" which had created serious distortions in the country's economic and political life. But in the late 1940s expanded military spending went hand-in-glove with the rise of an extreme anti-Communist campaign within the United States. In the new political climate, conservative politicians tried to reverse some of the social reforms of the New Deal era, and they were joined by liberal politicians in rallying the general public—including the labor movement—behind the pro-business foreign policy objectives.

The unions of both the AFL and CIO had gained a great deal from supporting U.S. foreign policy during World War II. It was clear that support for U.S. cold war policies would also bring benefits, while attempts to buck the tide would be detrimental to unions that had become dependent on a certain amount of governmental benevolence. This posed a problem for the CIO, in which Communists and other left-wing activists had played a significant role from the beginning.

The matter was further complicated by a deep contradiction in the modern Communist movement. Although Communist ideology called for the eventual replacement of capitalism with thoroughgoing rule by the whole working class over the political and economic life of society, the Soviet Union's dictator Josef Stalin (from the late 1920s to the early 1950s) headed one of the most bureaucratic and murderous tyrannies in human history. Mainstream Communists throughout the world—including their most selfless, effective, idealistic activists in the U.S. labor movement—defended that regime and loyally sought to harmonize their activities with its policies. At times, political consistency and even the interests of the workers were subordinated to Stalinist policy. This made it easier to victimize Communists, and to use the charge of "Communism" to smear or intimidate others who were critical of U.S. foreign policy. The anti-Communist clause in the Taft-Hartley Act was destined to play an important role in splitting the ranks of labor, and in domesticating the initially radical CIO.

The problem was brought to a head in 1948, when some radicals in the labor movement, including Communists, supported the new Progressive Party candidate for President, Henry Wallace. A onetime Vice-President under Franklin D. Roosevelt, Wallace made it clear that he was a firm supporter of the capitalist system—he simply wanted a return to New Deal reformism and an end to cold war policies. But all supporters of Wallace were savagely red-baited in the news media. No less importantly, the bulk of the CIO had committed itself to the re-election of Democrat Harry Truman, and once the elections were over, CIO president Philip Murray launched an attack to drive out the so-called left-led unions that had broken ranks in 1948. In the vanguard of this campaign to "drive the Commies out" was a former Socialist Party activist and the dynamic new president of the UAW, Walter Reuther.

Anti-Communists in the labor movement projected their efforts as a democratic crusade for a form of unionism better suited to advance the real interests of the average worker. Arguing that the CIO could not exist "part trade union dedicated to the ideals and objectives of the trade union movement, and part subservient to a foreign power," Reuther thundered: "You cannot work with people who are dishonest, who are devoid of the elemental, simple elements of decency and integrity, and these people by their record prove that they are bankrupt morally and that they are not interested in working honestly and sincerely and constructively with other decent trade-union elements." Some—like the militant Transport Workers Union president "Red" Mike Quill (who had once said, "I'd rather be called a Red by the rats than a rat by the Reds")—concluded that Communist Party policies "would either wreck the Communist Party within the CIO, or it would wreck the CIO," and switched over to the anti-Communist crusade so that the CIO, in Quill's words, "will no longer be run by a goulash of punks, pinks and parasites." A different view was expressed by James Matles of the "left-led" United Electrical workers. Bitterly commenting that "the cold warriors played a tune and the CIO danced to it, while the house of militant industrial unionism went up in flames," he lamented that "many leaders of the working class" had chosen to "give up the ghost of class struggle without a whimper" when they got "hooked on the drug of red baiting."

Forty years later, "labor priest" Monsignor Charles Owen Rice (who had been prominent in the Association of Catholic Trade Unionists and a leading participant in the anti-Communist purge) commented that the

Communists in fact "were good organizers technically and in terms of spirit, aggressiveness, and courage. They were, for the most part, on the right side of battles legislative and social" and "were good trade unionists . . . financially honest and dedicated." In a highly acclaimed history of the CIO, Robert Zieger—hardly uncritical of the Communist trade unionists—summarizes the historical evidence in a similar manner:

> The overall record of Communist-influenced unions with respect to collective bargaining, contract content and administration, internal democracy, and honest and effective governance was good. Rank-and-file Communists exhibited a passionate commitment to their conception of social justice. As a group Communists and their close allies were better educated, more articulate, and more class conscious than their counterparts in the CIO. . . . In regard to race and gender the Communist-influenced CIO affiliates stood in the vanguard.

In 1949 and 1950, eleven unions with a combined total of a million members were driven out of the CIO, charged with being Communist-dominated. All but two—the United Electrical, Radio, and Machine Workers of America (UE) and the International Longshore and Warehousemen's Union (ILWU)—were destroyed in the 1950s and 1960s by a combination of government persecution, employer attacks, media smears, and raids from anti-Communist unions that were happy to pick up already-organized union members. Left-wing workers who remained in CIO unions in auto, transit, maritime, and others, were generally driven from positions of influence, often through brutal factional fights, whether or not they were actually Communists.* (Years later, the still surviving UE and ILWU had reputations in labor circles for being among the more democratic, effective, inclusive, and socially conscious unions in the country. Some of the positive qualities among the "left-wing" unions were captured in the 1953 film *Salt of the Earth*—made by blacklisted motion picture employees—which movingly portrays racial and sexual divisions being overcome in a militant strike led by the "left-led" Mine, Mill and Smelter Workers.)

An architect of U.S. labor's foreign policy was Jay Lovestone, a former leader of the U.S. Communist Party—with a reputation, according to

---

* For example, one union devised its own loyalty oath which explicitly excluded "members of the Communist Party, the Industrial Workers of the World, or any Trotskyite group."

historian John Haynes, of having "considerable intellectual talent and a knack for ruthless factionalism"—who in the 1930s led a left-wing splinter group influential briefly in the UAW and more permanently in the ILGWU. By the late 1940s a de-radicalized Lovestone had gained the full confidence of leaders in the AFL (and, in later years, in the merged AFL-CIO). Describing the entire world Communist movement as consisting of "blind and mechanical followers," and Communist parties as "primarily para-military outfits organized to execute Kremlin commands," he warned: "As long as these people or parties remain loyal to the basic aims of Soviet communism or continue to place their faith in the principles of totalitarian communism, they cannot be anything else but apostles of totalitarian dictatorship—instruments of deceit, brutality and aggression." Lovestone and his closest associates worked with the U.S. State Department and Central Intelligence Agency in efforts to thwart revolutionary, left-wing, and Communist currents in the labor movements of Asia, Africa, and Latin America as well as Europe. Assisting moderate "pure and simple" trade unionists in various countries, Lovestone's policies were often criticized for helping to create weak unions more effective in transmitting Cold War propaganda than in defending workers' rights. But for many years to come such policies were not up for debate in U.S. labor's mainstream. Even some who were still associated with left-wing causes supported the anti-Communist foreign policy. Indeed, the staunchly reformist Socialist Party leader Norman Thomas and other like-minded figures in and around the labor movement, in a public statement explaining their "democratic social-ism" in the early 1950s during the Korean War, emphasized their belief that "the outstanding conflict today is between democracy, with all of its human and capitalist imperfections, and totalitarian despotism."

In fact, by this time distinctly left-wing and labor politics had pretty much dissolved into the liberal wing of the Democratic Party—or, as in the case of the Communists (whose 80,000 membership had melted to a fraction of their former strength), the Trotskyists, and the old IWW, had been marginalized almost to the point of irrelevance on the American political scene.

Labor's New Balance

The enforced conformity in labor's ranks resulted in a dramatic decline in the radical fervor and rough-and-tumble internal democracy that had been so vital to U.S. union growth in the 1930s. At the same time, it helped to narrow differences between the AFL and CIO. Since the late 1930s, many had referred to the rivalry between the AFL and CIO as "labor's civil war." Yet the split had unleashed the organizing fervor of the CIO and then, ironically, forced the AFL to modernize its own orientation just to catch up. By 1941 the AFL claimed 4.5 million members and the CIO 2.8 million, and in 1948 the AFL had 7.5 million and the CIO close to 6 million (though after the 1949–1950 purges this had dipped to less than 4 million). But in the early 1950s the rivalry—marked by public attacks and raids on each other's membership—was seen by increasing numbers of union leaders and activists as counterproductive, to say the least.

In 1952 the presidents of both federations, William Green and Philip Murray, had passed away. Ex-plumber George Meany took over as AFL president, and Walter Reuther of the UAW took over the CIO presidency. Meany was a cigar-chomping craft unionist who represented a dyed-in-the-wool "business unionism" far deeper than that of old man Gompers; he boasted: "I never went on strike in my life; I never ran a strike in my life; I never ordered anyone else to run a strike in my life, never had anything to do with a picket-line." Reuther's more youthful image was as an ambitious organizer with flair, a modern labor statesman who retained a taste for a more expansive social unionism, and he proclaimed that a unified labor movement would generate "an organization crusade to carry the message of unionism in the dark places of the South, into the vicious company towns, in the textile industry, in the chemical industry." The two new leaders engineered a merger which was consolidated in 1955, with Meany as president of the AFL-CIO.

Some saw the fusion as subordinating the militant social philosophy of the early CIO to what Transport Workers Union leader Mike Quill called the AFL's "three Rs—raiding, racketeering and racism." But Quill's hostility to AFL conservatism found little support among others. "The CIO had accomplished the work it set out to do, organizing the unorganized in the mass production industries," commented former CIO organization director John Brophy. "The zeal that the CIO put into its organization campaign energized the AFL and thousands of workers flocked into the old AFL unions as well." From this standpoint the merger made sense, and it brought together ninety-four affiliated unions with a combined membership of 15 million workers, approximately 36 percent of the labor force.

Some observers of the U.S. scene have noted that in the post–World War II period a "social compact" was forged between the three major forces in the economy—Big Business, Big Labor, and Big Government.* The "bigness" of labor was in the unprecedented size of union membership; the "bigness" of business was in the fact that a small percentage of the population owned colossal wealth and dominated the entire economy; the "bigness" of government involved the greatly expanded social-economic regulating functions and programs initiated by the New Deal, and even more the "military-industrial complex" that mushroomed with World War II and the cold war.

The "social compact" created by these forces meant that business would be free to grow in multiple ways, generating economic prosperity. The government would seek to create global "stability" through a foreign policy beneficial to U.S. business, and domestic "stability" through social programs that would defend U.S. business interests and economic and social security for the bulk of the population. Labor would accept the basic foreign policies of business and government, and the right of private business to own the economy, in exchange for high employment rates, paychecks, and fringe benefits that would yield rising living standards, and social programs that would give security to the young, to the unemployed, and to the elderly. This sense of well-being for many working-class families was enhanced by a market-driven consumerism that provided an increasing quantity of affordable, attractively packaged, alluringly advertised consumer goods to more and more people.

It is by no means the case, however, that businessmen in general embraced even the de-radicalized labor movement of the 1950s. As historian Elizabeth Fones-Wolf has documented, the "full-scale mobilization of business and conservative forces" launched in 1946 continued for decades afterward its sustained efforts to undermine and push back the power and influence of the labor movement through "lobbying, campaign financing, and litigation," as well as with probusiness propaganda.

---

* An astute labor historian, Mark McColloch, has argued that this government-mediated "social compact" can most realistically be seen as the outcome of a stalemate between the power of big business and the power of organized labor. Neither side could defeat the other, nor was it possible—given the nature of class relations and market dynamics—for either side to fully embrace the other. A long-term truce lasted until the 1970s, when the corporations began a process of outflanking their adversary.

This included "multimillion dollar public relations campaigns that relied on newspapers, magazines, radio, and later television to reeducate the public in the principles and benefits of the American economic system" in ways that glorified the large corporations while seeking to turn public sympathies against the alleged tyranny of "union bosses" and "government meddling." But the confrontation of business and the unions did not intensify—which is hardly surprising, considering that conditions in the affluent 1950s did not breed the crusading labor militancy of earlier years.

There were some old-timers, such as John Brophy in the AFL-CIO's Industrial Union Department, who believed in the need for "democratic planning for the common good," and who hoped that a unified and growing labor movement would "go forth to challenge the assumption of the business and financial group that they have a vested interest and a privileged position in the operation and management of industry, which they call 'free enterprise'; to extend our democracy to the economic field and to enhance the lives of the common people"—but such CIO rhetoric was largely the stuff of a bygone era.

"I stand for the profit system; I believe in the profit system. I believe it is a wonderful incentive," emphasized the AFL-CIO's new president. "I believe in the free enterprise system completely. I believe in the return on capital investment. I believe in management's right to manage." Asking U.S. businessmen "what is there left for us to disagree about," Meany answered: "It is merely for us to disagree, if you please, as to what share the workers get, what share management gets from the wealth produced by the particular enterprise." In an era of unprecedented productivity and business prosperity, it seemed clear that all could receive ample portions of the growing economic pie. Generous government social programs could easily be funded by taxing the expanding paychecks of America's affluent working-class majority. Any grievances at the workplace that remained could surely be ironed out with the help of government-appointed arbitrators, conciliators, and mediators.

As ex-socialist David Dubinsky, president of the International Ladies Garment Workers Union, explained: "Trade unionism needs capitalism like a fish needs water." The new "social compact" would mean, for the first time in history, that a majority of the U.S. working class would have a chance to realize "the American Dream."

CHAPTER 13

American Dream

The ethnic working-class enclaves and the labor-radical subculture that had been so important in the late nineteenth century and the first decades of the twentieth century had established certain patterns that impacted on the fortunes of the Knights of Labor, the AFL, and the IWW. But throughout the twentieth century profound shifts in economic and social reality, and in popular culture, were altering such patterns—reshaping working-class consciousness and powerfully affecting the nature of the labor movement. Labor ideology was also influenced by the effective employer assaults of "the American Plan" in the 1920s, the organizing needs among a culturally diverse workforce of the 1930s, the immensity of changes brought about by the war effort of 1941–1945, and the unprecedented postwar prosperity.

There developed a working-class "Americanism" that had both radical and conservative versions, but the ideology took its most common form as representing a rough cultural pluralism—the notion that all of America's ethnic groups could be accepted—combined with a conviction that there was the guarantee of a decent standard of living and upward mobility for those prepared to work for it, and a belief that elected politicians (imperfect as they might be) could more or less represent the will of the majority, with a general climate of freedom and well-being prevailing in this "best of all countries in the world." While some workers had been drawn to the socialist ideal of "rule by the people" over the economy, many more had what historian Liz Cohen describes as an "idealistic but nonetheless conservative economic loyalty to a 'moral capitalism'"—kept "moral" by the efforts of workers themselves. For many, unions were an essential ingredient in creating this type of "Americanism," and this ideology, especially

with the triumph of cold war anti-Communism, became the predominant outlook within U.S. trade unions of the 1950s and early 1960s.

Most important of all in changing the complexion of the U.S. labor movement were shifts taking place in labor-management relations and in the general economy by the early 1950s. Increasingly, wage raises were linked to rises in the company's productivity—making workers and employers "partners in progress," according to corporations' public relations departments. U.S. companies were experiencing previously undreamed-of profit margins—thanks to production innovations that caused productivity to soar, combined with the unprecedented long-range economic boom and the Number One position of the United States in the world economy. The companies, with government encouragement, were increasingly willing, in contract negotiations with the unions, to contribute to pension funds, social insurance, comprehensive medical benefits, extended vacation time, early retirement plans, plus higher wage levels than had ever been experienced by workers in U.S. history.

"Our members are basically Americans," explained George Meany about his AFL-CIO base in 1972. "They basically believe in the American system, and maybe they have a greater stake in the system now than they had fifteen or twenty years ago, because under the system and under our trade union policy, they have become 'middle class.' They have a greater stake."

Throughout the 1950s, 1960s, and into the 1970s, unions delivered the goods. The fact that more than one-third of the labor force was unionized gave the proponents of "business unionism" considerable leverage. Adjusted for inflation, average wages increased by 250 percent from 1945 to 1975. The rapidly expanding consumerism that this made possible—and which helped further stimulate economic growth—was further enhanced by financial innovations such as buying on credit, so that the relatively well-off working-class majority became more inclined to accept the status quo (and the "business unionism") that seemed to guarantee this version of "the American way of life."

Yet even at the height of its power, business unionism was problematical. Unions focused on negotiating over wages, benefits, and working conditions for their own members. Instead of being seen as an inspiring social cause of the entire working class, as was the case in the 1930s, or during the 1946 strike wave in many communities, organized labor came to be viewed more and more as a "special interest group" seeking benefits for a limited sector of the working class. Union members often spoke about the union not as if it was *themselves*, the organized workers who were joined together for their common interests, but rather as if it were an institution independent of them—like a social service agency or a law firm—that would either get or fail to get something for them from the companies.

Frank Marquait, a seasoned working-class radical who was for many years a labor educator in the UAW, linked this problem to the need for union democracy: "A union that is marked by tight control from above and the absence of membership participation in vital affairs is a sick union. In such a union a gulf develops between the leaders and the membership. The members become apathetic, indifferent, and even cynical. The life and vigor of the organization becomes dried up."* Marquart argued that "of all organizations, a union needs the invigorating influence of conscious participation on the part of the members. Only in this way can it be saved from bureaucratic dry rot." Internal democracy is naturally linked, according to Marquart, with the struggle for a more democratic society:

---

* Sociologist Donald Clark Hodges drew on his own experience as a factory worker in this period when he wrote that "cynicism...comes closest to expressing the informal philosophy of the workers," noting that this involves an attitude of those "disillusioned with the claims of anyone to better their conditions without profiting in the meantime at their expense." The consequent benefits enjoyed by union leaders could be simply material but could also be psychological and emotional. Onetime ILGWU labor educator Will Herberg (once prominent in the left-wing group led by Jay Lovestone but eventually turning to religious studies) wistfully reflected on "an element of self-seeking, hidden from himself though it may have been, in the idealist whose leadership in the cause served so frequently to inflate his pride and extend his power over his fellow-men."

The workers must identify themselves with their union by taking part in its activities, conflicts, internal struggles and worries. . . . If the workers cannot conduct their own organizations democratically and progressively, what hope is there that they will be able to pioneer beyond the day to day struggle for a few more cents an hour? . . . Unions should be training schools to fit the workers to struggle for a higher and better way of life. Only by actual participation in the task of running their own organizations can working people develop social vision and initiative.

Such radical democracy was powerfully resisted, however, by those in the upper levels of the union movement, including in organizations that had a reputation for favoring democracy and an expansive "social unionism."

Rank-and-file militants who had once used the unions to protest against low wages and miserable working conditions were viewed by many union leaders as a threat to the stability of the contract. Many workers who conducted "quickies" or wildcat strikes were fired by employers without union protest, and the decline of a culture of insurgency coincided with a steadily increasing speedup of the pace of work. Often union democracy evaporated, in some cases making possible abuses of power and the proliferation of corrupt practices by union officials. Frequently blown out of proportion by pro-business propagandists and the news media, such corruption was the target of congressional "antiracketeering" investigations.

One result of the focus on union racketeering was the passage of the Landrum-Griffin Act of 1959. Seen by many as a device to cut down Jimmy Hoffa, the aggressive and reputedly gangster-linked leader of the powerful Teamsters union, it was nonetheless opposed by sectors of the labor movement that were critical of Hoffa's corrupt practices. The new law had three key components: (1) the guarantee of a set of democratic rights for members within their unions, also enabling members to fight violations of such rights in court; (2) the empowerment of the federal government to regulate the internal affairs of unions in order to eliminate what government officials might view as coercive or corrupt practices; and (3) a toughening of certain provisions of the Taft-Hartley Act, further restricting picketing, secondary boycotts, etc. While some union dissidents and reformers would seek to use Landrum-Griffin provisions to advance their struggles, the law was generally seen as an antilabor measure, since it greatly expanded the power of the government to intervene in union affairs, a power that could be used as easily to undermine union democracy as to protect it. After all, the pro-business conservatives who flocked to support the bill were interested in enhancing "union democracy" to drive a wedge between union members and union leaders, not to enable a militant rank-and-file to become more combative against employers—and if the latter occurred, it was not inconceivable that the government would use its new intervention powers to "correct" the situation. In any event, the shift in labor's aura (in the media-influenced "public opinion") from the glow of social idealism to the taint of corruption justified this law in the minds of many, while the passage of Landrum-Griffin also signified for many union partisans an erosion of labor's power.

The fact remained that a majority of U.S. workers experienced significant gains in their living standards and economic security. In some cases unions got them these things. In other cases companies gave them these things in order to persuade employees that they didn't need unions. But there was something unique about the U.S. labor movement that was at the same time problematical. In Western Europe and most other industrial capitalist areas in the world, the organized labor movement was seen as having two major components: trade unions plus independent working-class political parties linked to the unions. This labor movement would seek to gain benefits for all working people: a national health plan for all, decent low income housing for all, good educational opportunities for all, unemployment insurance for all, etc. This was gained through national legislation that resulted in what was often termed "the welfare state" (of which Roosevelt's New Deal was only a pale version). In the United States, many of these benefits were not secured for workers through national legislation but through union contracts—and this left the majority of U.S. workers more vulnerable or in some cases completely unprotected. This would set the stage for the later erosion of gains won by unionized workers.

Management was left to decide how large the workforce would be, who would be hired, what would be produced, and how the economy would be shaped and reshaped. Management could build low-quality products and gouge consumers as long as union wages were paid to however many workers remained in the plant. Employers could make far-reaching decisions—utilizing new technologies, shifting plants to low-wage areas, shifting investments to other industries. This would—in the future—eventually eliminate hundreds of thousands of workers, pushing down the living standards that had been won not only through AFL-CIO business unionism, but also through hard-won struggles of earlier years. Automation or robotics—the linking of computers to industrial machinery to substantially eliminate the human laborer—posed many questions about the economic future. One Ford Motor Company executive taunted Walter Reuther, after a tour of an automated engine plant, with the comment: "You know, Walter, not one of these machines pays union dues." To which Reuther responded: "And not one of them buys new Ford cars, either." In the 1950s and 1960s, however, gloomy speculations about the future were not a primary consideration of most union members, who were doing quite well, especially since the beginning of automation did not (yet) create the large-scale unemployment that some had feared.

Another problem would develop in regard to labor's failure to develop an independent foreign policy orientation. Thanks to the "military-industrial" complex, federal largesse went to large weapons contractors such as General Electric, Lockheed, or General Motors instead of to programs that would build up the nation's infrastructure, housing, health, and educational needs. While spending on a large military and new weapon systems initially provided numerous jobs, the costs were quickly passed on to workers through higher taxes (after the 1950s, taxes on the wealthy and corporations were lowered)—not to mention the many thousands of workers in uniform killed in the Korean and Vietnam conflicts. Linked to this, the U.S. military supported the interests of corporations abroad. Governments in Latin America, Africa, or Asia that sought to do what the United States had done in the early 1800s—that is, to develop an economy independent of the already-industrialized countries—were often labeled "reds" or "anti-American" and punished. The U.S. government gave political, economic, and military support to numerous dictators who provided generous business climates for U.S. companies, and upstart governments like those in Guatemala, Iran, Guyana, Indonesia, and Chile were overthrown with decisive aid from the Central Intelligence Agency. Such policies were given the official AFL-CIO stamp of approval (and in some cases active assistance), although many of the more perceptive labor leaders and activists raised early and increasingly persistent cautions and criticisms.

CHAPTER 14

Unfinished Business

One of the most serious limitations of the U.S. labor movement was the failure to make good on the oft-repeated slogan: "Organize the unorganized." Operation Dixie, the effort launched in 1946 to organize the predominantly non-union Southern states, collapsed by 1948—and despite occasional flashes of rhetoric, it was never revived. Some argued that this would have required the type of crusading, class-struggle unionism, characteristic of the IWW or the CIO of the 1930s, that mainstream unions had turned away from. (It would also have involved a collision-course between labor and the Democratic Party—whose Southern standard-bearers typically lined up with wealthy employers.) The AFL-CIO of the 1950s and 1960s had the material resources but not the vision and deep commitment necessary to bring about the fundamental change in social and power relations a successful unionization drive would have represented. The region's conservative, antiunion, racist state governments remained intact as a powerful bulwark of traditional social and economic relationships. In fact, the number of Southern organized workers fell, and the South remained a non-union haven for runaway shops from the unionized North. It proved much easier throughout the country to increase the membership of one's union not through the kinds of efforts mounted in the 1930s, but by "raiding" the memberships of other unions—especially the "left-wing" unions expelled in 1949–1950, but also rival organizations within the AFL-CIO. Sometimes successful raids from outside of the AFL-CIO were also carried out against the federation's affiliates by the International Brotherhood of Teamsters—led by tough, dynamic, soon-to-be-murdered Jimmy Hoffa—which had earlier been expelled from the merged labor federation on racketeering charges. Some workers preferred the Teamsters despite charges of

corruption because it seemed to represent a tougher, more aggressive union than those in the AFL-CIO mainstream.

An important breakthrough in the 1960s and 1970s, on the other hand, was the spread of unionism among white-collar and service workers—such as government employees, teachers, and healthcare workers. This reflected changes in the U.S. occupational structure. Even within industry's increasingly automated workplaces, there were significant shifts from production to maintenance work—roughly by about 10 percent in the 15.5 million manufacturing workers. The high-growth sectors of the economy were in the white-collar and service sectors, and the high-growth labor organizations were now in these sectors: the Service Employees International Union; the American Federation of State, County and Municipal Employees; the American Federation of Government Employees; several organizations of postal workers; the American Federation of Teachers and the National Education Association; the Hospital Workers and a proliferation of nurses associations; etc.

There was more than simply the changing occupation structure at work, however. The 1960s and early 1970s also saw an upsurge of radicalization among young people challenging racism, poverty, war, conformist and authoritarian trends, sexual discrimination, and other social ills. The cultural and political ferment generated by the youthful activists found its way into workplaces and unions—especially as many of the activists themselves entered the job market.

Racism, Poverty, War

One of the most serious problems facing the United States, the U.S. working class, and the labor movement was the persistence of racism, which remained institutionalized in factories and within urban and regional labor markets. The systematic racial segregation imposed by law in the South, and the denial of voting rights, guaranteed that inferior living conditions and diminished opportunities would be available to African Americans there. But even in the North, blacks were subjected to segregated (and inferior) housing and schools, and fewer employment opportunities. This created serious problems for African American communities but also created a lower-wage sector that tended to pull down wages for all workers. Yet in some cases, black workers were locked out of union jobs through the joint agreement of management and the unions themselves. Even in some of the CIO unions, which had made a point of organizing blacks and whites together, many black unionists often had to fight their union and their company to win their seniority rights. By the 1970s, African American workers in some unions felt they had finally overcome the worst abuses, but as former steelworker Clarence Coe, a retired black unionist from Memphis, observed, "Before we left, blacks and whites were virtually equal; if you qualified for something, you could just about get it. But my God, man, when you'd given up thirty years of your life fighting for something that should've been yours to begin with, it's a little bit disheartening."

One of the foremost spokesmen for racial equality—criticizing the persistence of discriminatory policies within the labor movement—was A. Philip Randolph of the Brotherhood of Sleeping Car Porters. Another voice was provided by the Negro American Labor Council (a prestigious predecessor of the Coalition of Black Trade Unionists), which had members in a variety of unions. These were vital forces in the emergence of the early civil rights movement. A close associate of Randolph, E. D. Nixon of the Sleeping Car Porters in Montgomery, Alabama, helped initiate the successful Montgomery bus boycott of 1956, to which he recruited Rev. Martin Luther King Jr. While some white trade unionists were lukewarm or even hostile to the growing civil rights movement, others—mindful of the old union adage "an injury to one is an injury to all"—were supportive or even actively involved. Among unions around the country, in addition to the Sleeping Car Porters, that stood out in this regard were the UAW; the Amalgamated Clothing Workers; the United Packinghouse Workers; Hospital Workers Local 1199; the American Federation of State, County and Municipal Employees; the UE; and the ILWU. The impressive civil rights victories of the 1950s and 1960s inspired and benefited many working people. Yet it quickly became clear that these victories were not enough to solve the country's problems.

A growing number of labor activists recognized that racism could not be overcome unless bold new programs were developed to eliminate the underlying economics of inequality. It was recognized that developments in the U.S. economy generated technological and structural unemployment that was creating and maintaining a deep-rooted poverty which hurt a significant number of whites, but also an even higher proportion of African Americans, Hispanics, and other people of color. While the Democratic administrations of John F. Kennedy and Lyndon B. Johnson moved to wage a "War on Poverty," however, the effort was hampered by bureaucratic limitations and compromises with various conservative political forces in both political parties.

In 1966, A. Philip Randolph and others in the labor movement advanced—with the support of a broad array of liberal and progressive forces—an ambitious ten-year plan called *The "Freedom Budget" For All Americans* that would involve "abolition of poverty; guaranteed full employment; full production and high economic growth; adequate minimum wages; farm income equity; guaranteed incomes for all unable to work; a decent home for every American family; modem health services for all; full educational opportunity for all; updated social security and welfare programs; equitable tax and money policies." Many top

AFL-CIO leaders signed on to the "Freedom Budget." Civil rights leaders such as Martin Luther King also embraced this program, moving in the direction of supporting an interracial "poor people's movement" and progressive trade-union struggles. "The emergence of social initiatives by a revitalized labor movement would be taking place as Negroes are placing economic issues on the highest agenda," King commented. "The coalition of an energized section of labor, Negroes, unemployed and welfare recipients may be the source of power that reshapes economic relationships and ushers in a breakthrough to a new level of social reform."

Such a far-reaching social program was beyond the scope of either the Republican or Democratic parties, which were not inclined to challenge the more conservative and narrowly profit-minded priorities established by the big corporations that controlled the country's economic resources. Since labor did not have a political party of its own, this closed the door on such proposals as the "Freedom Budget." Randolph acidly noted that the persistence of poverty and racism were rooted in "fundamentally economic problems which are caused by the nature of the system in which we live. This system is a market economy in which investment and production are determined more by the anticipation of profits than by the desire to achieve social justice."

The Vietnam War provided a more traditional way to stimulate the economy and to employ young men seeking to escape the cycle of poverty. At the same time, it drew government dollars away from more serious programs designed to overcome the sources of poverty. The cost of the war strained the economy and added to the tax burden of working-class taxpayers. Hundreds of thousands of Americans and millions of Vietnamese were killed and maimed in the effort to prop up an unpopular right-wing dictatorship that embraced U.S. foreign policy goals and business interests. While the AFL-CIO supported the war until its end, by the early 1970s, several unions and many union members had grown disillusioned with the war and what seemed to many an unpersuasive policy of knee-jerk anti-Communism. The massive antiwar protests (among whose organizers was the old labor educator and radical pacifist Rev. A. J. Muste) were the first since World War I to attract the support of sizable numbers of trade unionists, as increasing numbers of Americans questioned the value of this brutal war for the majority of the U.S. and Vietnamese people.

Economic Slippage, Labor Unease

By the late 1960s, the U.S. economy was feeling the initial effects of a period of profound economic crisis (which would—by the early 1970s—finally translate into a reversal of the capacity "business unionism" to generate rising working-class incomes and living standards). The United States began to run up small deficits with its trading partners. This had less to do with "high" labor costs than with the high costs of the cold war. Military spending had provided full employment during World War II and the Korean War, but in the long run, money spent on the military was not invested in socially useful ways, and in particular there was a failure to develop the country's economic infrastructure and to invest in modernizing technology. U.S. industrial development began to lag behind advances in Japan, West Germany, and other countries where military spending was a fraction of that in the United States. As profitability slipped, companies began to search for new ways to pad their bottom lines. In the 1940s and 1950s, American companies exported manufactured goods to less industrialized countries, providing jobs to U.S. workers. But by the 1960s, U.S. companies had eliminated many jobs through automation and also began to shift manufacturing to cheap labor areas overseas, where unions and radical workers groups had been severely weakened. Thus the AFL-CIO's orientation of supporting U.S. foreign policy had helped to provide low-wage sites for runaway shops from the United States.

The failure of the War on Poverty, the persistence of economic and racial inequality, the erosion of workers' economic security and the mounting tax burden on the middle-income working class, the tensions created by civil rights and antiwar protests, and the failure of the AFL-CIO leadership to offer decisive leadership around a progressive social and political program that would inspire and benefit the country's working-class majority—all of this led to working-class fragmentation and disorientation. A rift opened up between a frustrated Walter Reuther of the UAW and the majority AFL-CIO leadership around George Meany, with Reuther insisting in early 1967 that "the American labor movement, if it is to fulfill its destiny and become the vanguard of social progress, must restore its sense of purpose and direction, instill vitality, imagination and initiative in its programs and their accomplishment and be imbued with the dynamic spirit of social responsibility." In the following year, the UAW withdrew from the AFL-CIO to establish, with rhetorical flourishes worthy of a better product, what turned out to be a still-born Alliance for Labor Action with the previously expelled Teamsters and the relatively small International Oil and Chemical Workers union. (It wasn't until the 1990s that the UAW, Oil and Chemical, United Mine Workers, and a democratized and reformed International Brotherhood of Teamsters found their way back into the AFL-CIO.)

Within the UAW ranks, however, the development of groups such as the Dodge Revolutionary Union Movement (DRUM) arose in 1968 to challenge the union leadership's progressive image. With articulate leaders who blended radicalized black nationalism (influenced by Malcolm X) with Marxism and ideas of Chinese Communist Mao Tse-tung, the dissidents targeted what they saw as the UAW leadership's backwardness both on the need to combat racism and the need to develop a class-struggle union policy. Winning significant influence among young black autoworkers, nonetheless the challengers failed to build a durable base in the union. Other less dramatic dissident currents in various unions—some far less radical, others rooting their radicalism more effectively in the actual experience of other workers—also flourished throughout the 1960s and 1970s, but with the partial exception of the Miners for Democracy movement that finally dislodged a corrupt (post–John L. Lewis) machine in the United Mine Workers of America, they enjoyed minimal gains. Not long afterward, however, in the gangster-ridden International Brotherhood of Teamsters there arose a caucus dedicated to militancy, a broad social vision, and union democracy—Teamsters for a Democratic Union—which began a fundamental reform process that would help transform one of the nation's largest labor organizations over the next two decades.

The absence of an effective and dynamic strategic orientation within the labor movement did not stop workers from seeking solutions outside of the unions for the problems they faced. But they weren't all looking in the same places. Some white workers shifted toward political conservatives claiming to offer solutions that seemed beyond the grasp of Democratic Party liberals—leading to a partial blue-collar migration toward the Republican Party. At the same time, many African Americans, Hispanics, women, and young people were inclined to organize around issues having to do with what they saw as their own special oppression. Some youthful activists contributed to a partial revitalization of older left-wing groups, while many more—animated by an energetic idealism though sometimes also exasperating political immaturity—created a vibrant cluster of "new left" groups and an even more widespread radical "counterculture." And yet many of these activists were, in fact, an integral part of the working class, and some were soon to be central to the rapid growth in union membership in the healthcare, government, and education sectors of the economy.

Much of this development was foreseen by some of the more perceptive labor activists. Cleveland Robinson—the Secretary-Treasurer of the left-oriented District 65 of the Retail, Wholesale and Department Store Union (and A. Philip Randolph's successor as head of the Negro American Labor Council)—pointed out in 1967 that "the unorganized are to be found, in the main, among the 70 percent of the nation's work force who are not industrial workers but service workers" that the AFL-CIO had up to the 1960s been inclined to ignore. A high percentage of these workers were made up of African Americans and other people of color. Internal democracy in unions that recruited such workers was essential, Robinson insisted, in order to create "unions whose program will respond to our needs, unions which will be a force to be reckoned with." Because of neglect and discrimination, many in the black community had become distrustful of unions. Robinson and many other African American trade unionists believed—as he put it—that it was necessary "to bring home to the masses of our people the basic truth that unions are essential, and that in a large sense it is the people, the workers themselves, who really make the union."

Stirrings

Below the upper echelons of the AFL-CIO, new currents in the labor movement to some extent recaptured the expansive idealism and radical spirit of previous years. Cesar Chavez played an important role in combining many elements—a pride in the heritage of Mexican Americans; the shrewdness of community organizing efforts of the 1960s; the commitment to social justice of the Catholic Church; the perspective of alliance-building among Chicano, Filipino, and other agricultural workers; and the vision of a socially conscious unionism appealing to the general public (through grape and lettuce boycotts)—elements that were essential to building the United Farm Workers of America. "As a continuation of our struggle," Chavez said, "I think we can develop economic power and put it into the hands of the people so they can have more control of their own lives, and then begin to change the system. We want radical change." The fighting spirit sometimes personified by the late John L. Lewis permeated such groups as the Black Lung Association and Miners for Democracy that helped to revitalize the United Mine Workers of America. In the United Auto Workers, the United Steelworkers, the Teamsters, and other unions a proliferation of rank-and-file caucuses and reform campaigns sometimes won victories and sometimes endured defeats, but contributed a new militancy and awareness of social issues, helping to regenerate the ranks of organized labor in the era of the Nixon-Ford presidencies.

The spirit of Mother Jones, Rose Schneiderman, Elizabeth Gurley Flynn, and so many other heroines of early labor struggles was also to be found in the growing role of women in the workplace and union movement. Increasing numbers of women—including many in so-called nontraditional industrial jobs, in mines and steel mills and auto plants—helped to change the face of labor. Historians Brigid O'Farrell and Joyce Kornbluh—highlighting the concept of "union feminists"—point out that while "the contemporary women's movement helped influence union women to support equal rights," it is no less the case that "union women helped influence the women's movement to address other important issues in working women's lives, such as pay equity, a higher minimum wage, child care, and health and safety on the job, that came from the realities of their day-to-day experiences." Some organized the Coalition of Labor Union Women as well as caucuses in their own unions, in part to help push forward women's concerns and women's role in the ranks of organized labor. They also played key roles in the general struggles of the working class, and some were on the cutting edge of such struggles. One famous female activist was Dolores Huerta, the eloquent and inspiring organizer who became a key leader of the United Farm Workers. Explaining that over time it became evident in the farm workers' struggles that "women are stronger than men," with "more staying power," Huerta explained the importance of not allowing dangerous aspects of the struggle to be restricted to men:

> Excluding women, protecting them, keeping women at home, that's the middle-class way. Poor people's movements have always had whole families on the line, ready to move at a moment's notice, with more courage, because that's all we had. It's a class, not an ethnic thing.

Another well-known female union activist was Karen Silkwood, who helped to unionize her atomic-processing factory in Oklahoma. Horrified by her company's lax environmental standards, Silkwood was on her way to a meeting with reporters when she became the victim of a mysterious car accident. (This new type of "union maid" was even depicted in Hollywood films, such as *Norma Rae* and *Silkwood*).

Although unions like the United Steelworkers; the Oil, Chemical and Atomic Workers (Silkwood's union); and others had pressed Congress to establish the Occupational Safety and Health Act in 1970, the agency was never adequately funded even in the 1970s. In the 1980s, OSHA was targeted as a heavy-handed antibusiness bureaucracy by corporations worried by a new round of working-class organizing.

In fact, the business community was about to launch a broad and far-reaching offensive of its own, designed to push against working-class gains in order to tilt power relations dramatically back in their own favor. Nor was the challenge to be met by any dynamic new personalities (not to mention visionary union leaders with effective strategies) who might have become prominent in the unions' upper echelons after the passing of the two dominant figures of the post–World War II period. Walter Reuther had died in an airplane accident in 1970, and no one of equal stature was able to strike as effective a pose as champion of social unionism. The 1980 retirement of George Meany left his assistant Lane Kirkland in the AFL-CIO presidency. Meany's distinctive gruffness proved a hard act to follow, even though his policies were loyally maintained. But the effectiveness of those policies were increasingly open to question under the changing conditions.

CHAPTER 15

Rude Awakenings

To understand the reasons for the business "get-tough" policy toward workers in the 1970s and 1980s, it is important to understand the success of one aspect of U.S. foreign policy in the post–World War II period: the goal of rebuilding the economies of war-torn Europe and Asia on a firm capitalist basis, with the apparent assumption that the United States would continue to be the economic leader of the "Free World." By the 1970s and 1980s, it was clear that in a sense this policy had become too successful—to the detriment of U.S. "Number One" status in the world economy. Other industrial nations, especially West Germany and Japan, were becoming more competitive, contributing to the growth of a U.S. trade deficit. U.S. businesses sought more profitable operations, and among the ways to achieve this were: (a) move factories to cheap-labor areas in the "third world"; (b) shift investments away from less profitable (and higher-wage) industrial sectors; and (c) drive down labor costs and production costs in U.S. industries.

Labor's Position in the Changing Economy

Corporations set out to change the rules of the game that allowed workers to unionize, raise their wages, and/or clean up their workplaces. While corporations had always lobbied for tax breaks or subsidies, new organizations like the Business Roundtable advanced a broad agenda designed to lower labor costs of the working class as a whole. A media and political campaign was waged to convince the public that deregulation would benefit consumers and that workers' wages (rather than corporate investment patterns) were leading to U.S. economic decline.

This media campaign was given power by the fact that factories *were* closing. Beginning in the mid-1970s and continuing through the

1990s, industries central to the economy, such as steel, auto, mining, and shipbuilding, all lost hundreds of thousands of jobs. Hundreds of factories were closed by global corporations like General Motors, General Electric, and U.S. Steel. A broad range of organizations and efforts in places such as Youngstown, Ohio (the Ecumenical Coalition of the Mahoning Valley, the Mahoning Valley Economic Development Committee, Steelworkers United for Employment, the Save Our Valley Campaign, Local 1462 of the United Steelworkers) and Western Pennsylvania (the Mon Valley Unemployed Committee, the Tri-State Conference on Steel, the Denominational Ministry Strategy, the Save Dorothy Campaign, Locals 1397 and 1256 of the United Steelworkers) fought hard in the early 1980s to prevent steel mill shutdowns, to establish worker-community ownership and control over threatened mills, to reverse the dismantling of industry in their areas, and to aid the thousands of workers and their families who suffered the effects of the decision by the corporations to shift away from steelmaking to more profitable ventures. Throughout the United States, working-class communities were devastated and the former center of heavy industry stretching from the Midwest to the Northeast was labeled the "rust belt." What's more, under the banner of fighting against "welfare cheats" and of lifting the burden from the middle-class taxpayer, many social programs beneficial for the most impoverished sectors of the working class were targeted for substantial cuts and eventual elimination.

Some of these changes began under the administration of Democratic President Jimmy Carter. Carter initiated deregulation policies which were a boon to corporate profiteering, at the same time initiating increasingly deep cuts in social programs to the detriment of the less fortunate layers of the working class, and overseeing the beginning of a downturn in middle-income living standards. Such things enabled the conservative Republican Presidential candidate Ronald Reagan to look into the eyes of many working people and ask: "Are you better off or worse off now than you were four years ago?" The negative answer to that question helped to elect Reagan President of the United States. With his running mate and successor, George Bush, Reagan led the reorientation to a modern-day form of laissez-faire economic policies that further devastated social programs and further empowered already powerful multinational corporations.

Reagan also led the way in breaking the power of unions—beginning with the dramatic destruction of the Professional Air Traffic Controllers Organization (the jailing of its leaders, and the firing of 11,500 of its members)—and ushered in a new era in which more than four decades of social reforms began to be dismantled root-and-branch. Unions found it difficult to increase wages and benefits in the new atmosphere, in which corporations, the news media (owned by corporations), and the corporate-friendly federal government all demanded that unions engage in "concession" bargaining, and many—succumbing to the threat that plants would close otherwise—provided "give-backs" in the form of generous wage and benefit cuts. The Reagan administration supplemented this with generous tax cuts for big business and the lifting of various government environmental and health and safety regulations that corporations had long complained about.

The so-called Reagan Revolution was supported by many in the working class because they hoped that it would bring a return to better times for those who were willing to work hard. Deep government budget cuts were—according to government spokesmen—supposed to help the taxpaying public, with special consideration given to the big corporations that would utilize tax breaks in order to modernize their plants, which would have a "trickle-down" effect by creating more jobs and prosperity for all. Instead, in each year of the 1980s, about 2 million workers lost their jobs due to plant closings or permanent layoffs; of these, more than 25 percent remained unemployed, and 33 percent of those lucky enough to find new jobs lost 20 percent or more of their previous earnings. While top corporate executives in 1960 made 41 times the wage of the average factory worker, by the 1990s they made 187 times the wage of an average worker. Throughout the 1980s, corporate profits rose 205 percent, while the wages of production workers rose slower than the price rise in consumer goods. While in the 1950–1978 period family income in all sectors had grown, in the 1979–1994 period the bottom 60 percent of all families saw their inflation-adjusted incomes decline. By 1989, 20 percent of U.S. families owned 80 percent of the wealth (with the top 1 percent actually owning 40 percent), while the bottom 80 percent of U.S. households was left with only 20 percent of the wealth.

As the *Philadelphia Inquirer*'s Pulitzer Prize-winning journalists Donald Bartlett and James Steele summed it up in 1992, "the already rich are richer than ever; there has been an explosion in overnight new rich; life for the working class is deteriorating, and those at the bottom are trapped." While in 1959 the country's richest 4 percent had the same income ($31 billion) as the bottom 35 percent, and in 1970 the richest 4 percent had the same income as the bottom 38 percent, by 1989 the income of the wealthy 4 percent (now $452 billion) was equivalent to that of the bottom 51 percent. The inequality was also reflected in tax cuts for the rich—for example, the average tax bill for millionaires fell 27 percent from 1986 to 1889. Several years later, Bartlett and Steele commented: "America's largest and most powerful businesses now pay federal income tax at a fraction of the rate they once paid. . . . If corporations paid federal income tax in 1996 at the effective rate paid in the 1950s, the U.S. Treasury would collect an extra $250 billion a year—wiping out the federal deficit overnight. The top corporate rate in the 1950s was 52 percent. In the 1990s, it's 36 percent." The declining tax share shouldered by big business translated not only into a bigger tax burden for working-class taxpayers, but also in deepening cuts in spending for health, education, public services, and social "safety net" programs important to the working class as a whole.

U.S. Position in the Global Economy

Government policies favoring U.S. multinational corporations facilitated the development of innovations in communications and technology that made it increasingly easy for the corporations to shift manufacturing, marketing, and investments from one part of the globe to the other, and this "global restructuring" of the economy gave U.S. multinational corporations increasing leverage over workers here and throughout the world. Business media sources persistently and often gloatingly proclaimed that unions, strikes, and collective bargaining were obsolete, and that the labor movement was about to go the way of the dinosaur and the woolly mammoth. Decisive defeats of a number of hard-fought strikes—among workers at Phelps-Dodge, Greyhound, and Trans World Airlines—lent credence to such propaganda. (A lesser-known fact was that thousands of attorneys and consultants throughout the country were being paid many hundreds of millions of dollars by big corporations for the purpose of fighting and destroying unions, leading to the question: "If something is dying out anyway, why spend so much money to kill it?")

In addition to getting tough with labor on the domestic front, the Reagan administration initiated a new round of cold war tensions with the Soviet Union, justifying an enormous increase in military spending at the same time that he was cutting social programs. Both Republicans and Democrats (with few exceptions) also backed the Reagan-Bush escalation of U.S. involvement in Central America, supporting right-wing dictatorships and military forces—guilty of massive human rights abuses—in order to drive back combined peasant, working-class, Christian, and left-wing insurgencies in the region. The result was the preservation of cheap-labor areas that could be used as profitable "free trade zones" (free of taxes, regulations, and unions) for U.S. investors.

President Bush's continuation of these policies failed to reverse the declining U.S. economic position in the global economy, as technologically more modernized countries—Germany and Japan in particular—surged forward in European and Asian trading blocs that threw into question how long "the American Century" would actually last. The decline was compounded through massive damage done to the U.S. economy by irresponsible corporate traders in the Savings and Loan scandal, which the federal government moved in to clean up—vastly increasing the U.S. debt shouldered by working-class taxpayers. Sagging economic clout and tarnished prestige were offset by the Bush administration when it mobilized a multinational military effort in the Persian Gulf; this was in response to aggressive moves toward oil-rich Kuwait by the government of Iraq. A quick and easy victory, the U.S.-orchestrated war against Iraq emphasized which country was still the Number One military power on the planet—but this did not translate into any quick and easy solution for the nation's economic woes.

And yet, the U.S. economy did pull ahead of the German and Japanese economies in certain significant respects. From 1982 to 1990, real hourly wages and benefits (adjusted for inflation) fell by 3.5 percent in the United States, while rising 18.4 percent in Japan and 26.9 percent in Germany. In the same period, U.S. manufacturing workers' productivity kept pace with or did better than U.S. business's key competitors: the United States achieved a 36.6 percent productivity increase, compared with 38.1 percent for Japan and 24.8 percent for Germany. The result was that the United States was the only major economic power to see a drop in unit labor costs during the 1980s—a fact that was very good for corporate profits, but which meant that U.S. employees were working harder for less. In fact, 25 percent of all full-time workers spent forty-nine or more hours a week on the job in 1990, almost half of these working sixty hours or more. What's more, there was a dramatic increase in the so-called contingent workforce made up of part-time, temporary, or contract workers. Involving between 30 and 40 million people, the "contingent" workforce was mostly non-unionized, working for low wages and with minimal or no benefits, often for long hours. This added up to a growing cheap-labor source that further undermined the economic situation of all workers.

The weakened position of the U.S. working class is reflected in the decline of union membership from close to 36 percent of the labor force in 1955 to about 14 percent in 1995. The decline in the struggle for higher wages can be charted in declining strike statistics: unions in the 1950s averaged 352 work stoppages a year, and in the 1960s averaged 289; the 1980s yearly average fell to 83; the first half of the 1990s saw an annual average of 38.

By the mid-1990s a team of researchers headed by Kate Bronfenbrenner noted that "without the restraining power of unions, corporate leaders have been emboldened to expropriate an ever-larger share of profits for themselves. Fifty years ago, executives were paid forty times the earnings of average workers; today's executives' salaries are more than two hundred times those of workers."

New World Order?

In the late 1980s and early 1990s, President Bush and others celebrated the birth of a "New World Order" as Communist regimes in Eastern Europe and the Soviet Union collapsed under the weight of their own bureaucratic inefficiency and from active popular resentment against their dictatorial practices. Also contributing to the Communist collapse was the escalation of the cold war arms race by the Reagan-Bush administrations (at the expense of U.S. cutbacks in social programs), an escalation which greatly weakened the USSR's economy as it sought to match the astronomical military expenditures. Worth mentioning, too, is the fact that Western business loans to Eastern European governments made their economies vulnerable to the international economic downturns of the 1970s and 1980s.

"Free market" propagandists insisted that the fall of the Communist dictatorships proved the superiority of capitalism's market economy and that a truly wonderful future would now be molded by visionary executives of "high-tech" corporations. But most of the working class didn't see this rhetoric translated into reality. Instead hard-nosed economists and hard-hearted employers stressed the need for businesses to become "lean and mean," even if this caused "regrettable" but necessary "pain" for working people. (Much of this is reflected in Michael Moore's savagely hilarious film on the General Motors Corporation's abandonment of Flint, Michigan, *Roger and Me*). Declining living standards and cuts in benefits continued to be experienced by those working in a variety of occupations. Corporate "downsizing" increasingly inched its way up from blue-collar to white-collar sectors, and even middle managers found themselves pulled downward to the unemployment lines.

CHAPTER 16

Where To, What Next?

In the face of the growing power of big business during the last half of the twentieth century, partly accomplished through accelerating corporate mergers and economic restructuring, unions in the United States felt compelled to go through their own process of mergers and restructuring.

For example, the "left-led" Fur and Leather Workers union was absorbed by the Amalgamated Meatcutters and Butcher Workmen, which combined with the Packinghouse Workers to go into the increasingly huge United Food and Commercial Workers. The Amalgamated Clothing Workers combined with the Textile Workers and later merged with the International Ladies Garment Workers Union to form UNITE—the Union of Needletrades, Industrial and Textile Employees. The United Steelworkers absorbed the United Stone and Allied Products Workers; the "left-led" Mine, Mill and Smelter Workers; District 50 of the United Mine Workers; the United Rubber Workers; the Upholsterers International Union; and the Aluminum, Brick and Glass Workers; at the close of the 1990s it was engaged in three-way merger talks with the United Auto Workers and the International Association of Machinists. At the same time, the American Federation of Teachers and the National Education Association were considering a possible merger that would create the biggest union in the country.

On the face of it, the trend appeared to be going in the direction of the old IWW ideal of "One Big Union" that would combine the power of all workers. But questions could be raised about the extent to which union members would have a genuine voice and exercise democratic control within these increasingly huge organizational structures. Related to the future success of the labor movement—no less than the issue of

union democracy—was the question of what strategy and tactics would be pursued by the restructured unions.

In this period it was the blue-collar working class that fought back most impressively. In the 1970s Douglas Fraser, then head of the UAW, had angrily accused the big corporations of initiating "a one-sided class war" against workers. By the 1980s it was clear that the class struggle had become two-sided once again.

Labor Fights Back

New tactics were employed by some unions: campaigns focused public attention on the greed, arrogance, and authoritarianism of the big corporations. This tactic was utilized effectively to supplement militant strikes, but was sometimes employed less effectively as a substitute for mass mobilizations of the workers to shut down production. On the cutting edge of the new struggle was the truly heroic fight against "concessions" launched by United Food and Commercial Workers Local P-9 in 1987 against the Hormel Corporation, a fight which the UFCW leadership concluded was "unwinnable" and attempted to end, severely undercutting the Local P-9's struggle and splitting the workers. There were similar efforts elsewhere to combine a strike with an anticorporate campaign—inspiring considerable enthusiasm and support, but sometimes not ending in victory due to the companies' ability, thanks to legal restrictions on strikers, to use scabs (or "replacement workers") to keep production going.

The high point in the union struggles of this period came in 1989 with the massive mobilization, from the top leadership on down to the humblest member, of the United Mine Workers of America—and not only miners, but also their families and friends, and many allies—to stop operations at the Pittston Coal Corporation by any means necessary. Typically dressed in army camouflage, union partisans waged more or less nonviolent guerrilla warfare that relentlessly challenged company spokesmen, unfair labor laws, anti-union court orders, scabs, thugs, police, and whatever else the bosses threw at them. And they won a resounding victory. When workers were able to hold together, secure the full support of their union leadership, mobilize their communities, build alliances with other workers, and wage a truly militant and uncompromising mass struggle, they had a chance of winning.

The example of working-class struggle was followed by members of the United Steelworkers of America in Ravenswood, West Virginia. After five workers died on the job at the Ravenswood Aluminum Company, 1,200 workers there targeted unsafe conditions in a militant 1992 strike, supplemented by a corporate campaign (aggressively educating and mobilizing public opinion against company abuses) and tough pressure in the courts from the union's legal staff. The Ravenswood workers scored another victory for labor.

Other workers also fought back, and while success was never guaranteed, some felt deeply that the dignity of working people could only be secured by refusing the path of quiet submission. In 1992, workers in Local 7837 of the United Paperworkers International Union launched an inspiring struggle when the A. E. Staley Manufacturing Company in Decater, Illinois attempted to impose a twelve-hour workday on top of the steady and deadly erosion of workplace safety. It was a long, bitter strike, with countrywide travels by teams of eloquent strikers (nicknamed "road warriors") to build strike support among other workers. The struggle was punctuated by militant confrontations and mass arrests, as the strikers and their allies did all that they could to reverse the company's assault on their living and working conditions. But they were finally overwhelmed by a combination of factors: an enormously powerful British-owned corporate conglomerate, an indifferent-to-hostile news media, the so-called law-and-order forces of a government dominated by pro-business elements, the failure of the larger labor movement to mobilize effectively and decisively, and the eventual erosion of many strikers' ability to continue the fight.

Politics

With no strong and consistent political voice or force of its own in the electoral arena, labor found itself seriously hampered in defending its rights. And yet, major political figures have taken the power of the working-class vote very seriously. In 1992, Democratic presidential candidate Bill Clinton recognized the growing discontent among working people—his campaigners' slogan among themselves was, "It's the economy, stupid." While it wasn't clear who "stupid" was supposed to be, Clinton was swept to victory. Yet the government, with a Democratic administration and a Democratic-controlled Congress, remained firmly pro-corporation. In 1993, President Clinton and the congressional majority diluted, warped, and then totally fumbled a popularly desired healthcare reform that would provide decent medical care to all people as a matter of right. Nor were they able to generate much energy to carry out labor-law reforms that would benefit the working class. But they proved admirably resolute, and quite successful, in efforts to further deregulate and "internationalize" U.S. labor markets by passing, with full Republican cooperation, the North American Free Trade Agreement (NAFTA) and General Agreement on Trade and Tariffs (GATT).

As increasing percentages of disgusted and disillusioned voters stopped going to the polls, because they didn't see significant differences between the two major parties, Republicans were able to take control of Congress for the first time in decades. The Republican majority pushed forward a conservative "Contract with America," much ballyhooed in the mass media, that would further dismantle the post–World War II social compact, junking many gains of the civil rights era, and explicitly targeting reforms won in the New Deal era, as well. The Republican program enhanced the authority, power, and profits of "the market" and "the private sector," that is, of big business. Many Democrats, sometimes including President Clinton, made it clear that they saw merit in much of the Republican program. "Welfare as we know it" was eliminated through both parties working together—and many middle-income workers applauded the elimination of what they felt was a heavy tax burden. But it was not clear that there would be jobs for the less fortunate bottom layers of the working class being thrown off the welfare rolls.

The existence of growing and increasingly desperate cheap-labor sectors of the U.S. workforce would certainly pull down wages, living standards, and the quality of life for the working class as a whole.

Many dedicated labor activists concluded, in the 1996 presidential election, that they had little choice but to continue to support the Democratic Party, which they felt would be less antilabor than the Republicans. But a higher percentage of workers registered, in many ways, a profound dissatisfaction with "politics as usual." Many didn't even bother to register to vote in elections that they felt would make no difference in their lives, and less than half of those registered actually voted. Calls for an independent labor party were heard within the ranks of organized labor—particularly as the loose network of Labor Party Advocates won significant union support to carry out more aggressively the old labor appeal to "educate and agitate and organize."

The Changing Face of U.S. Labor

But the nonelectoral sphere saw an even greater variety of efforts to transform organized labor, which had shrunk by the late 1980s to include less than 15 percent of the workforce. A number of organizations and informally organized currents had come into being to help the movement meet the needs of working people at the dawn of a new century: Justice for Janitors; Black Workers for Justice; the Farm Labor Organizing Committee; the Chinese Staff Association; Jobs with Justice; the biyearly conferences of the monthly publication *Labor Notes* drawing thousands of union activists; various working-class community centers; efforts to form international alliances among union members of different countries; and a proliferating number of reform caucuses working, often successfully, for more democracy and militancy and social consciousness in their unions.

Such efforts helped to transform the labor movement, a transformation that at the AFL-CIO's 1995 convention generated a powerful challenge to the "business unionism as usual" orientation represented by outgoing AFL-CIO president Lane Kirkland. A "New Voices" slate was put forward and elected with John Sweeney of the Service Employees International Union as president, Linda Chavez-Thompson of the American Federation of State, County and Municipal Employees as executive vice-president, and Richard Trumka of the United Mine Workers of America as secretary-treasurer. The new leadership explicitly identified with the impressive ferment and the powerful mobilizing techniques that were bringing new life to the labor movement.

"A revitalized labor movement will offer working Americans a way to win better pay, benefits, conditions, and opportunities—even in the face of attacks from powerful corporations," Sweeney argued. "The challenge is to find ways for working people to support each other in their struggles and to use media coverage, political clout, community organizing, international support, and even pressure from investors and major customers to persuade employers to come to terms."

It remains to be seen to what extent all of this will lead to an effective new orientation for the labor movement, and to the qualitative improvement of the lives of the working-class majority that constitutes 80 percent of the population of the United States. Some critics have argued that what the new AFL-CIO leadership does *not* represent—at least not yet—is an "organizing model" of unionism that is rooted in the actively democratic involvement of its membership at the local level, as opposed to a "service model" of unionism that is based on the union staff (under the direction of the national officers) providing services to more or less passive members who are mobilized on special occasions. On the other hand, from the beginning the new leadership expressed a commitment to create ongoing organizing, educating, and mobilizing centers involving members and activists on the local level through a "Union Cities" strategy that would revitalize a network of central labor councils in urban areas throughout the country.

In advancing this aggressive new orientation, however, the unions faced a powerful adversary in the large business corporations. As veteran sociologist Patricia Cayo Sexton bluntly summed up the realities at the beginning of the 1990s, "the excessive and repressive powers of U.S. economic elites" had caused "perilous distortions . . . in the American economy and in the whole fabric of society," especially with "the class war they have conducted against labor for well over a century." She explained and documented that the antilabor strategies "have included the use of private and public armed force against unionism, dominance of the mass-media, the stigmatizing of much labor-left activity as 'un-American,' manipulation of the legal system and labor relations, control of economic policy and the globalization of the U.S. economy, and especially the heavy influence brought to bear on government policy and on a political system that is uniquely inhospitable to challenges from the labor-left." Public opinion is often pulled in an anti-union direction, Sexton pointed out, "when only twenty-six corporations control more than half the media communications that reach well over 200 million Americans." Labor's side of the story often receives short shift, while "conservative views are distributed to the public via the business-owned mass media—a media more tightly controlled by big business than in any comparable democracy." Similarly, "investors, not voters, now control American politics, Democratic and Republican, and they overwhelmingly support candidates and legislation favoring economic elites." According to Sexton, massive infusions of corporate campaign contributions had "shifted largely to conservatives in both parties." The new AFL-CIO efforts to buck this tide were bound to have repercussions.

In late 1997, conservative news commentators and politicians launched a media and legal assault to discredit the new breed of labor leaders, charging that many of them were guilty of seeking too much power and of improper financial dealings regarding funds for the campaigns of union reformers as well as prounion electoral candidates. Such alleged misdemeanors were widely denounced—especially by employers uneasy about militant strikes and Republicans indignant over union money going to Democrats—as prime examples of "union corruption." (Ironically, in earlier years the once gangster-dominated Teamsters' union had enjoyed a cozy relationship with conservatives in the Republican Party.) There were no similar protests by conservatives regarding the far bigger financial contributions to political candidates coming from big-business sources.

It would be a mistake, however, to reduce controversies over the "New Voices" orientation in the AFL-CIO simply to petty partisan politics. More fundamental ideological issues are at stake, as well as basic questions about the economic and political future of the U.S. working class.

Some commentators have argued that the new orientation of the labor movement will not be successful because the dramatic "high-tech" transformation of the increasingly globalized economy has made this sort of thing obsolete—that efforts to recapture the militant spirit of the old labor movement represent little more than a desperate last gasp. Max Green, a former union staffer for New York's United Federation of Teachers (and onetime leader of the Young People's Socialist League) who became a financial and investment advisor associated with the conservative American Enterprise Institute, asserted that the new economic reality now "makes unions irrelevant" and this causes them to be "increasingly disaffected from American capitalism." The AFL-CIO had, in his opinion, "degenerated into a left-wing interest group," but Green was convinced that "the decline of American labor is destined to continue" no matter who is in charge.

Some believers in capitalism's future, however, also continued to believe that there remains a future for the labor movement as well—but only by turning away from "New Voices" radicalism. Far from creating adversarial confrontations, it was asserted, one must realistically adjust to the trends being set by the multinational corporations in order to take advantage of new opportunities in the twenty-first century. The AFL-CIO should be a vehicle for "gradual social change as opposed to a vehicle for class warfare," as Jonathan Mahler—a firm partisan of returning to the old Meany orientation—argued in the pro-business *Wall Street Journal*. Mahler looked hopefully to a resurgence of a moderate "business unionism" through coalition between centrist-to-conservative intellectuals and "the so-called bread and butter unions . . . which are primarily concerned with wages, pensions and benefits."

It is doubtful, however, that the "New Voices leadership actually wanted a policy of class warfare. As President John Sweeney asserted at the 1997 AFL-CIO convention: "One of our paramount goals is to help the companies we work for succeed, to work with our employers, to creatively increase productivity and quality and to help American companies compete effectively in the new world economy and create new jobs and new wealth for our families and communities to share." This suggests that the new AFL-CIO militancy fostered by "New Voices" was part of a strategy to build up the labor movement for the purpose of forcing business and government into a new 1950s-style "social compact" that will once again enable a majority of U.S. workers to reach out for the American Dream. But some critics questioned whether the "New Voices" effort could be carried out effectively enough to accomplish even this relatively modest goal. Would the AFL-CIO leadership actually be willing to commit itself to the patient organizing, deep-going rank-and-file democracy, and militant struggles which are necessary for making the union federation a powerful force? Radical labor activist and writer Kim Moody warned that "a top-down method of operating and organizing characterized by media flash, technique, big spending, and a fundamentally bureaucratic approach to problems that leave the unions as they are, . . . will fail even in terms of the officialdom's own priorities."

Some argue that the labor movement must go even further in the direction of an expansive social unionism—developing a labor ideology that constitutes "a work-centered way of seeing the world," moving decisively beyond a consumption-oriented "what's in it for me" outlook that pits various workers, factories, unions, and communities against each other. Instead, a need is felt to develop an orientation that draws various sectors and components of the diverse working class into a dynamic but unified whole. Thus labor educators Michael Yates and Fernando Gapasin (in the socialist magazine *Monthly Review*) have written of a need, as they put it,

> for an ideological alternative for the labor movement that unabashedly champions unifying class themes: every worker has the right to a decent job; every worker has the right to publicly funded health care, education at all levels, daycare, paid family leaves, and vacations; racism and sexism must be eradicated now; every institution in society must be democratically controlled, including workplaces, unions, and all levels of government; work must become an end in itself and not just a means to the end of more private consumption; workers everywhere in the world are exactly the same as those here, and must have the same rights. And it must be admitted clearly that our economic system is utterly incapable of satisfying these demands.

This appears to add up to nothing less than what might be called "a third American revolution"—that of 1776 ending the rule of kings over the United States, the second ending the existence of chattel slavery, and the third ending the power of wealthy corporations in order to consolidate a radically democratic social order.

The balance struck by the AFL-CIO leadership at the close of the twentieth century seemed poised between the sophisticated business unionism of midcentury America and the radical social unionism of earlier years—but this was in the face of economic challenges unique in U.S. history. At the dawn of the twenty-first century it was obvious that the new balance of organized labor was only transitional. It remains to be seen to what extent the promise of democracy—rule by the people—will become a living reality in the new century. The great poet Carl Sandburg, in his epic of the 1930s, *The People, Yes*, asked who can live without hope, and affirmed optimistically that time is a great teacher.

Bibliographical Essay

The first edition of this book had a bibliographical essay of more than twenty pages. Here, I offer something updated but also more succinct. Additional sources can be found in the first edition and also in bibliographies of works listed here.

Companion Volumes

A close companion volume to this one has now come out in its own second edition, by my friend Michael Yates, titled *Why Unions Matter* (New York: Monthly Review Press, 2009). This is a handy, well-written resource that combines history, sociology, economics, and political science. The two books, read together, reinforce each other—just as the friendship of the two authors gave strength and insight to each.

Given that this book offers a *short* history of the U.S. working class, some readers may want to turn their attention to additional books that offer more detail. Different facets of labor's story are drawn together in a variety of accounts.

Jeremy Brecher focuses on labor insurgencies from the bottom up in his classic *Strike!*, Revised, Expanded, and Updated Edition (Oakland, CA: PM Press, 2014), while Paul Buhle focuses on top-down bureaucratic labor conservatism in *Taking Care of Business: Samuel Gompers, George Meany, Lane Kirkland, and the Tragedy of American Labor* (New York: Monthly Review Press, 1999).

Patricia Cayo Sexton chronicles the repressive anti-labor efforts of the powerful in *The War on Labor and the Left: Understanding America's Unique Conservatism* (Boulder, CO: Westview Press, 1992), while Sharon Smith gives a sense of unquenchable struggle in *Subterranean*

Fire: A History of Working-Class Radicalism in the United States (Chicago: Haymarket Books, 2006).

Bill Fletcher Jr. provides a set of capable refutations to anti-labor arguments in *"They're Bankrupting Us!" and 20 Other Myths about Unions* (Boston: Beacon Press, 2012), while Stanley Aronowitz weaves personal and scholarly reflections into a rumination on how future labor victories might be won in *The Death and Life of American Labor: Toward a New Workers' Movement* (London: Verso, 2014).

Broader Contexts

It makes sense to consult general histories of the United States to contextualize the experience and development of the U.S. working class. One of the most succinct, but quite good, is Paul Boyer, *American History: A Very Short Introduction* (New York: Oxford University Press, 2012). A longer, very readable account can be found in Eric Foner, *Give Me Liberty! An American History*, Fourth Edition (New York: W. W. Norton, 2013). A now classic left-wing synthesis is Howard Zinn, *A People's History of the United States* (New York: HarperCollins, 2005). A richly multi-cultural tapestry highlighting the intersection of class and ethnicity is Ronald Takaki's beautifully written *A Different Mirror: A History of Multicultural America* (Boston: Little Brown, 2008).

It also makes sense to consider the historical dynamics of the economic system and labor process. Louis M. Hacker's *The Triumph of American Capitalism* (New York: Columbia University Press, 1947), while certainly dated, has never quite been surpassed. Much is added, in various ways, by such studies as Bruce Levine, *Half Slave and Half Free: The Roots of the Civil War*, Revised Edition (New York: Hill and Wang, 2005); Paul A. Baran and Paul M. Sweezy, *Monopoly Capital: An Essay on the American Economic and Social Order* (New York: Monthly Review Press, 1966); Harry Braverman, *Labor and Monopoly Capital: The Degradation of Work in the Twentieth Century* (New York: Monthly Review Press, 1998); and David M. Gordon, Richard Edwards, and Michael Reich, *Segmented Work, Divided Workers: The Historical Transformation of Labor in the United States* (New York: Cambridge University Press, 1982).

The centrality of the political left to the history of U.S. labor has been veiled all too often, but this does a disservice to those who seek to understand what actually happened in history. A useful resource on the history of the U.S. left is Mari Jo Buhle, Paul Buhle, and Dan Georgakas, eds.,

Encyclopedia of the American Left, Second Edition (New York: Oxford University Press, 1998).

Classics

Several older classic works on the U.S. labor movement are worth exploring. The first is a two-volume study by the experienced and insightful German-American associate of Karl Marx, Friedrich Sorge: *Labor Movement in the United States: A History of the American Working Class from Colonial Times to 1890* (Westport, CT: Greenwood Press, 1977) and *Labor Movement in the United States: A History of the American Working Class from 1890 to 1896* (Westport, CT: Greenwood Press, 1987).

The work of ex-socialist Selig Perlman is an especially valuable component of John R. Commons and his coeditors (David J. Saposs, Helen L. Sumner, E. B. Mittelman, H.E. Hoagland, John B. Andres, Selig Perlman, Philip Taft) in *History of Labor in the United States*, 4 volumes (New York: Macmillan, 1918–1935).

An attempt to compose a Marxist version of the work of Commons et al. can be found in Philip S. Foner, *A History of the Labor Movement in the United States*, 10 volumes (New York: International Publishers, 1947–1994).

Louis Adamic's *Dynamite: The Story of Class Violence in America* (Oakland, CA: AK Press, 2008) surveys certain dynamics that add important dimensions to the story.

It may be reasonable, here, to draw attention to the work of U.S. labor historians who provided especially important examples to me as I engaged with the history of the working class.

One such scholar was my teacher, David Montgomery, whose works included: *Beyond Equality: Labor and the Radical Republicans, 1862–1872* (New York: Alfred A. Knopf, 1967); *Workers' Control in America: Studies in the History of Work* (New York: Cambridge University Press, 1982); *The Fall of the House of Labor: The Workplace, the State, and American Labor Activism, 1865–1925* (New York: Cambridge University Press, 1987); and *Citizen Worker: The Experience of Workers in the United States with Democracy and the Free Market during the Nineteenth Century* (New York: Cambridge University Press, 1995).

Some of Herbert Gutman's most marvelous work is gathered in two volumes of essays: *Work, Culture and Society in Industrializing America* (New York: Alfred A. Knopf, 1977) and *Power and Culture: Essays on the American Working Class*, edited by Ira Berlin (New York: Pantheon Books, 1987).

David Brody's books focused on the early twentieth century—*Steelworkers in America: The Nonunion Era* (Urbana: University of Illinois Press, 1987) and *Labor in Crisis: The Steel Strike of 1919* (Urbana: University of Illinois Press, 1987)—but his more wide-ranging essays are gathered in three volumes: *Workers in Industrial America*, Second Edition (New York: Oxford University Press, 1993); *In Labor's Cause: Main Themes on the History of the American Worker* (New York: Oxford University Press, 1993); and *Labor Embattled: History, Power, Rights* (Urbana: University of Illinois Press, 2005).

Also worthy of mention is Melvyn Dubofsky, whose *We Shall Be All: A History of the Industrial Workers of the World* (Urbana: University of Illinois Press, 2000), *Industrialism and the American Worker 1865–1920* (Arlington Heights, IL: AHM Publishing, 1975), and essays in *Hard Work: The Making of Labor History* (Urbana: University of Illinois Press, 2000) have exerted strong influence.

From the 1930s to 2000

For the triumph of industrial unionism in the 1930s, readers can consult Irving Bernstein, *The Turbulent Years: A History of the American Worker, 1933–1941* (Chicago: Haymarket Books, 2010), Art Preis, *Labor's Giant Step: The First Twenty Years of the CIO, 1936–1955* (New York: Pathfinder Press, 1972), and Robert H. Zieger, *The CIO, 1935–1955* (Chapel Hill: University of North Carolina Press, 1995).

The accounts of Preis and Zieger go through the 1940s and conclude in the 1950s with the AFL-CIO merger. An outstanding study of the 1940s by George Lipsitz, *Rainbow at Midnight: Labor and Culture in the 1940s* (Urbana: University of Illinois Press, 1994), marks the first phase of that era, and the story is taken into the 1950s and 1960s with Lizabeth Cohen, *A Consumers' Republic: The Politics of Mass Consumption in Postwar America* (New York: Vintage Books, 2003). The interplay of Communism and anti-Communism in all of this is discussed in different ways in two intelligent and informative works—Len De Caux, *Labor Radical: From the Wobblies to the CIO, A Personal History* (Boston: Beacon Press, 1971) and Bert Cochran, *Labor and Communism: The Conflict that Shaped American Unions* (Princeton: Princeton University Press, 1977)—and in Judith Stepan-Norris and Maurice Zeitlin, *Left*

Out: Reds and America's Industrial Unions (New York: Cambridge University Press, 2002).

Studies on developments of the late twentieth century include two fine works by Michael K. Honey—*Southern Labor and Black Civil Rights: Organizing Memphis Workers* (Urbana: University of Illinois Press, 1993) and *Going Down Jericho Road: The Memphis Strike, Martin Luther King's Last Campaign* (New York: W. W. Norton, 2008)—as well as Peter B. Levy, *The New Left and Labor in the 1960s* (Urbana: University of Illinois Press, 1994); Paul Le Blanc and Michael Yates, *A Freedom Budget for All Americans* (New York: Monthly Review Press, 2013), Aaron Brenner, Robert Brenner, and Calvin Winslow, eds., *Rebel Rank and File: Labor Militancy and Revolt from Below during the Long 1970s* (London: Verso, 2010); and Kim Moody, *An Injury to All: The Decline of American Unionism* (London: Verso, 1988).

Focal Points

Focusing on laboring women are works by Barbara Mayer Wertheimer, *We Were There: The Story of Working Women in America* (New York: Pantheon Books, 1977) and Alice Kessler-Harris, *Out to Work: A History of Wage-Earning Women in the United States* (New York: Oxford University Press, 2003). Also important is Rosalyn Baxandall and Linda Gordon, eds., *America's Working Women: A Documentary History, 1600 to the Present*, Revised Edition (New York: W. W. Norton, 1995). A rich collection of oral histories can be found in Brigit O'Farrell and Joyce L. Kornbluh, eds., *Rocking the Boat: Union Women's Voices, 1915–1975* (New Brunswick, NJ: Rutgers University Press, 1995). A valuable assortment of scholarly essays is provided by Ruth Milkman, ed., *Women, Work and Protest: A Century of U.S. Women's Labor History* (New York: Routledge, 2014).

Studies of the African-American working-class experience include William Harris, *The Harder We Run: Black Workers since the Civil War* (New York: Oxford University Press, 1982), Philip S. Foner, *Organized Labor and the Black Worker, 1619–1981* (New York: International Publishers, 1982), Jacqueline Jones, *American Work: Four Centuries of Black and White Labor* (New York: W. W. Norton, 1998), and Robert H. Zieger, *For Jobs and Freedom: Race and Labor in America since 1865* (Lexington: University Press of Kentucky, 2007). For a documentary collection, see Philip S. Foner and Ronald L. Lewis, eds., *Black Workers: A Documentary History from Colonial Times to the Present* (Philadelphia:

Temple University Press, 1988). Collections of scholarly essays are available in Joe Trotter, Earl Lewis, Tera Hunter, eds., *The African American Urban Experience: Perspectives from the Colonial Period to the Present* (New York: Palgrave Macmillan, 2004), and Eric Arnesen, ed., *The Black Worker: Race, Labor, and Civil Rights since Emancipation* (Urbana: University of Illinois Press, 2007). A scholarly-activist blend of past and hoped-for future is presented in Manning Marable, Immanuel Ness, and Joseph Wilson, eds., *Race and Labor Matters in the New U.S. Economy* (Lanham, MD: Rowan and Littlefield, 2006).

In the fascinating *Rebels, Reformers, and Racketeers: How Insurgents Transformed the Labor Movement* (self-published, 2004), ninety-year-old labor militant Herman Benson draws on decades of experience to focus on how efforts to reform the labor movement can transform it into a vibrantly democratic, inclusive, and effective force. A similar focus, with many practical tips, can be found in Mike Parker and Martha Gruelle, *Democracy Is Power: Rebuilding Unions from the Bottom Up* (Detroit: Labor Notes, 1999).

A massive and rich focus on strikes—analyzing reasons for past defeats and victories—can be found in the informative Aaron Brenner, Benjamin Day, and Immanuel Ness, eds., *The Encyclopedia of Strikes in American History* (New York: Routledge, 2009).

The Past Flows into the Future

Those of us with a life in two centuries—born in the twentieth, but coping with realities of the twenty-first—may have a keener sense than others of how the past flows into the future. If we have lived long enough, we have seen amazing changes.

Two capable histories of U.S. labor in the century in which we were born—Robert H. Zieger and Gilbert J. Gall, *American Workers, American Unions* (Baltimore: John Hopkins University Press, 2002) and Nelson Lichtenstein, *State of the Union: A Century of American Labor* (Princeton, NJ: Princeton University Press, 2002)—may help to ground us in what went on before today.

But scholars must have a sense of the present in order to make sense of the past, just as activists need to comprehend new realities if there is any hope of making use of such understanding of the past. In this, we may be helped by the spate of new works, such as Immanuel Ness, *Immigrants, Unions, and the New U.S. Labor Market* (Philadelphia:

Temple University Press, 2005), Bill Fletcher Jr. and Fernando Gapasin, *Solidarity Divided: The Crisis in Organized Labor and the New Path toward Social Justice* (Berkeley: University of California Press, 2009), and Kim Moody, *In Solidarity: Essays on Working-Class Organization and Strategy in the United States* (Chicago: Haymarket Books, 2014).

Spirit and Creativity

As scholars seek to comprehend the past, they can be helped by listening to the voices of those who engaged in making the history that is now being studied. As activists cope with the present and struggle for a better future, they can find empowerment through interaction with those who were engaged in past efforts to make their way in life, and to struggle for dignity and justice.

The spirit of those who labored and struggled in times long passed can be found in the words they left behind. There are different works that enable us to hear those voices. Studs Terkel, in his book *Working: People Talk about What They Do All Day and How They Feel about What They Do* (New York: The New Press, 1997), helps us listen to a rich variety of women and men, with diverse work and life experience, while Staughton and Alice Lynd, eds., *Rank and File: Personal Histories by Working-Class Organizers*, Second Edition (Chicago: Haymarket Books, 2012) set down the reminiscences and reflections of experienced labor activists who made history in the 1930s and later. In Paul Le Blanc, *Work and Struggle: Voices from U.S. Labor Radicalism* (New York: Routledge, 2010), we can learn from speeches and writings of freedom fighters associated with the working class—Tom Paine, Frederick Douglass, "Mother" Mary Jones, Eugene V. Debs, Fannia Cohn, A. Philip Randolph, Genora Dollinger, Cesar Chavez, and others.

Such voices can also be heard in innumerable creative works—poems and songs, short stories, novels, reminiscences—such as those represented in the more than 900 pages of Nicholas Coles and Janet Zandy, ed., *American Working-Class Literature: An Anthology* (New York: Oxford University Press, 2006).

The men and women and children from the past come to life for us through images as well—photographs and creative artwork—in books such as those that can be found in William Cahn, ed., *A Pictorial History of American Labor* (New York: Crown Publishers, 1972), Richard B. Morris, ed., *The U.S. Department of Labor Bicentennial History of the American Worker* (Washington, DC: 1976), and Joyce Kornbluh, ed., *Rebel Voices: An IWW Anthology* (Oakland, CA: PM Press, 2011). Only the third title is in print—perhaps some day the living past will be returned to us with new editions of the first two (for which it is still worth searching libraries and rare book dealers).

There are also motion pictures—documentaries and fictional presentations—which convey some of labor's rich and multi-faceted story, and 350 of these are identified in Tom Zaniello, *Working Stiffs, Union Maids, Reds, and Riffraff: An Expanded Guide to Films about Labor* (Ithaca, NY: ILR Press/Cornell University Press, 2003).

Glossary

affirmative action—policies designed to facilitate employment or advancement of those traditionally subjected to discrimination (such as ethnic or racial minorities and women).

AFL (also A.F. of L.)—American Federation of Labor.

AFL-CIO—the merged American Federation of Labor and Congress of Industrial Organizations, which came into being in 1955.

American Federation of Labor—a federation of unions that was established in 1886 (with a predecessor, the Federation of Organized Trades and Labor Unions, formed in 1881).

American Plan—a post–World War I offensive by employers to combat unionism.

anarchist—wants a society without bosses, where people run things without a government. While "anarchy" is commonly understood to mean chaos and confusion, the anarchist uses the word to indicate a different goal—a relatively harmonious, self-governing society in which freedom reigns.

apprentice—a person learning a craft or skilled trade; after serving an apprenticeship, this person becomes a journeyman.

arbitration—when a union and company are unable to settle a dispute and refer the issue to someone who is supposed to be a neutral third party who listens to both sides and then makes a decision (that is usually binding for both sides).

artisan—independent skilled worker, generally self-employed.

assembly line—a beltline on which workers assemble a product, each one performing small task in a process resulting in a finished product. An essential innovation in the development of mass production industries in the early twentieth century, this involved a combined de-skilling and intensification of labor that gave the employers and their managers greater control over the labor process while at the same time spectacularly increasing productivity and profits.

automation—involving technological innovations at a workplace, in which human labor is replaced by electronically run and often computerized equipment.

bargaining unit—a specified group of workers who bargain collectively with their employer.

blacklist—a secret list, shared by employers, of union members, radicals, or others who may be considered "undesirable"; those on the list are excluded from employment.

blue-collar worker—worker engaged in manual or physical labor in factories, mines, construction, transportation, etc.

boycott—refusal to buy certain products; used by unions to pressure businesses that are fighting against unions. Also may involve a union's refusal to handle goods that are the focus of a strike—such as the refusal of the American Railway Union to handle Pullman cars during the 1894 Pullman strike.

bureaucracy—the functioning of administrative hierarchies and routines for the purpose of governing and regulating complex social entities. Bureaucracies are very pronounced in most major institutions in modern society: government agencies, large-scale businesses, etc. They function supposedly to enhance efficiency and accountability, but they often are seen as concentrating excessive power in a few hands while also—for those at the bottom of the hierarchy or outside of the bureaucratic apparatus—replacing cumbersome and fixed routines for intelligent judgments. There is controversy over the extent to which managerial bureaucracies remove control of business corporations from their owners (many social scientists have concluded that top managers and top stockholders are closely interlinked), but such bureaucracies certainly represent an increase of powerlessness for a company's employees. It has also been argued that, especially with the development of "business unionism," union bureaucracies have in many instances smothered a sense of democratic participation by the memberships of various unions.

business—serious activity. Often referring to a profit-making enterprise, it can also refer to all businessmen or capitalists.

business agent—a union official who handles workers' grievances, organizes new workers, bargains with employers, etc. The term is most commonly associated with AFL unions; CIO unions more often use terms such as "organizer" or "representative."

business unionism—a narrowly focused form of unionism, embracing the capitalist system and focusing on improving wages, hours, working conditions, etc. for the union's membership.

capital—the money that is used to open or run a business; the machinery and material in which such money is invested; the products of such a business; the money made from the sale of these products. When one is speaking of "labor and capital" the term refers to all businessmen (or capitalists).

capitalism—an economic system in which the economy is privately owned, more or less controlled by the owners, and utilized for the purpose of maximizing profits for the owners; it involves generalized commodity production—that is, it draws more and more aspects of life into a buying-and-selling economy (or market economy). The most dynamic economic system in history, it has gone through a number of stages—sometimes given such labels as commercial capitalism, industrial capitalism, corporate capitalism—and has over and over again transformed the labor process, the working class, all of society, and the world.

capitalist—a business person, some one making a living through the ownership of a capitalist enterprise, generally of a large-scale.

central labor council—a city or county federation of local unions that are affiliated to various national or international unions.

CIO—Congress of Industrial Organizations; prior to 1938, Committee for Industrial Organization.

class—a sector of the population defined by its relationship to the economy; broader than the concept of "occupation." For example, the working class includes people who work in many different occupations.

class collaboration—a far-reaching form of worker/capitalist cooperation that turns away from the notion of class conflict and is generally based on the acceptance of capitalism.

class struggle—ongoing antagonism, tension, and conflict between classes, particularly workers and capitalists.

CLC—Canadian Labor Congress. Some international unions with members in the United States and Canada today are affiliated both with the AFL-CIO and the CLC.

closed shop—a workplace where only union members can be hired—workers must join the union before being employed. Illegal under the Taft-Hartley Act.

cold war—a major confrontation—between Communist-ruled countries led by the Soviet Union (particularly Russia) and capitalist countries led by the United States, between 1946 and 1990—involving military buildups and arms races, political and economic pressures and counter-pressures, covert and small-scale conflicts, and massive propaganda, even relatively small military clashes (such as in Korea and Vietnam), but not total (hot) war.

collective bargaining—when representatives of the union and company discuss wages, hours, working conditions, etc. and then write what they agree on into a contract.

commerce—business involving buying and selling.

commercial capitalism—a form of capitalism that is essentially based on commerce, buying and selling goods, as opposed to producing goods (which is industrial capitalism); also called "mercantile capitalism."

commodity—something produced for the purpose of selling it.

Communism—holds that society, not businessmen, should run and benefit from the economy. Over the centuries there have been many variants of communist theory, the most modern being a form of revolutionary socialism associated with the views of Karl Marx and with the 1917 Russian revolution led by V. I. Lenin, which later degenerated into a brutal dictatorship under Josef Stalin. The term has therefore had opposite connotations for different people—as something either representing or destroying freedom and democracy.

company—a business.

company store—a store set up by a company for its employees, who are often forced to buy only from that store, generally at higher prices.

company town—a town set up by a company for its employees, generally placing them under greater control of their bosses.

company union—a phony union set up and controlled by a company for its employees, to prevent a real union from being organized.

Congress of Industrial Organizations—a federation of industrial unions which emerged from the AFL and became independent in 1938; it merged with the AFL in 1955 to form the AFL-CIO.

conservative—someone who is inclined toward traditional ways of doing things, often wanting to preserve existing power relationships.

consumerism—a cultural development related to the mass production and mass marketing techniques arising in industrial capitalist countries during the twentieth century, in which a majority of people in society are powerfully oriented toward buying more and more consumer goods (often as a substitute for other, more meaningful orientations involving freedom, creativity, a sense of community, etc.).

contract—a written agreement between unionized workers and a company regarding the rights and obligations of each (including wages, hours, working conditions, etc.) which is to govern their working relationship for a set period of time—often one, two, or three years.

corporation—the primary form of business ownership under modern-day capitalism, which facilitates the amassing of larger investment capital and also provides various legal and financial protections to the owners. The ownership of the business is divided into a number of shares of stock that are bought by various people (stockholders) who regularly receive a share of the profits equivalent to the amount of stock they own; each share also enables them to vote on policies and for officers of the corporation (although a small number of big stockholders invariably have a controlling interest). The dominant corporation today is the *multinational corporation* (sometimes called transnational corporation) which has extensive operations in a multiple number of countries.

corruption—degeneration from the original intentions, goals, or nature of something.

cost-of-living index—the Consumer Price Index prepared by the U.S. Labor Department, measuring changes in the cost of living month by month and year by year.

craft—a job requiring much skill and experience.

craftsman—a person who works at a craft (sometimes economically independent, sometimes employed by someone else).

craft union—a union organized along lines of specific skilled crafts.

culture—having to do with the way of life of a society or group of people, including political and economic dynamics, customs and family patterns, religions and values, ideologies or ways of understanding reality, education, ways of relating to people, creative and artistic expressions, etc.

democracy—a form of government involving rule by the people.

depression—an economic downturn involving large-scale business failures and massive unemployment.

discrimination—unequal treatment because of race, sex, religion, nationality, union membership, etc.

downsizing—laying off employees, then forcing the workers who remain to increase their output in order to make up for the diminished workforce.

dual unionism—an orientation of creating and maintaining a separate trade union, for either ideological or practical reasons, that competes with an already-existing trade union. The IWW and CIO were both accused by the AFL leadership of "dual unionism" that would split the ranks of organized labor (although both of these AFL rivals, representing a more expansive social unionism than the "pure and simple" orientation dominating the AFL, also stood for the unionization of unskilled mass-production workers largely ignored by the old AFL).

dues—a sum paid regularly for membership in an organization to which one belongs; union dues have been essential in paying for a union staff (organizers, negotiators, etc.), offices and meeting halls, strike funds, leaflets and newspapers, and other things required by a cohesive and substantial organization.

dues checkoff—a clause in many union contracts authorizes the employer to deduct union dues from employees' paychecks and turn them over to the union. Some argue that this greatly enhances the financial stability of the union, others that it contributes to a decline in contact between union members and the organization representing them.

economy—the activities and relationships people enter into, and the resources they rely on in order to get the things that they need and want.

elitism—the belief (and policies flowing from the belief) that some people are better than others and therefore entitled to greater decision-making power and/or more benefits and opportunities than the others.

escalator clause—a clause in a union contract providing for automatic cost of living raises in workers' pay to keep pace with rising consumer prices, usually measured by the Consumer Price Index.

ethnic group—a group of people at least partly set off from others because of an identification with a distinctive regional or national origin, and who share at least some elements of a common cultural background. There have been many such groups in the U.S. working class—often fragmenting a common sense of class consciousness—who identify as Irish American, Polish American, Italian American, African American, Chinese American, Mexican American, etc. Often different ethnic groups have been discriminated against, concentrated in one or another segment of the occupational structure, excluded from better paying jobs, denied membership in specific unions. Sometimes ethnic groups have been termed "races" and have been subjected to racist bigotry. Ethnic divisions were often utilized by employers to establish greater control over the workforce, at the same time undermining solidarity within the ethnically diverse working class—although the labor movement was strengthened whenever such divisions were transcended.

exploitation—has the connotation of taking unfair advantage of someone; many unionists argue that this exists whenever workers are underpaid; labor radicals generally argue that capitalists *always* exploit workers because the source of all value—including profits—is labor.

factory—a workplace which brings together substantial amounts of machinery, raw materials, and labor.

Fair Employment Practices Committee (FEPC)—set up by the U.S. government during World War II to eliminate discrimination in hiring and pay based on race, creed, and national origin.

fink—derogatory term for a worker not loyal to the union, who informs on fellow workers to the employer; originated as "pink," derived from "Pinkerton" (the latter term referring to the detective agency hired to break strikes and send company spies into labor organizations).

Fordism—a term to indicate techniques associated with pioneering automobile manufacturer Henry Ford, and generalized in the U.S. economy, involving assembly-line production to increase control over the labor process and increase productivity at the same time lowering prices, while at the same time increasing wages and other benefits in order to undercut unionization and to stimulate consumption of these mass-production goods.

free enterprise—capitalism.

free trade—involves the free movement of capital (whether as investments, raw materials, or finished products) without high tariffs or other restrictions.

fringe benefits—gains in addition to wages that are negotiated for workers, such as paid vacations and holidays, health benefits, insurance, pensions, supplemental unemployment benefits, etc.

general strike—a strike of all workers in a town, city, region, or country. This involves a major power confrontation between workers and employers (and often the government as well) and if successful results in a major shift in power relations. It is seen as having revolutionary implications. (Related to, but distinct from, the notion of a more spontaneous "mass strike" development.)

globalization—the capitalist system has always been dynamically expansive and innovative, with an aggressively global reach in its quest for markets, raw materials, and investment opportunities. Some analysts argue that since the 1980s it has been undergoing a process of transformation—which they refer to as "globalization"—in which developments in technology, communications, and transportation have caused economic expansion to transcend national frameworks more dramatically than before, enabling multinational corporations to rise above any restraints or impositions that national governments or labor movements may wish to establish. This shift in power relations, according to these analysts, has resulted in dramatic increases in corporate profits but makes it difficult to prevent the deterioration of working-class living standards and the dismantling of "welfare state" reforms of the past.

goon—a violent strong-arm man brought in to break strikes and unionization efforts.

grievance—a contract violation or abuse on the job which, under union contracts, a worker can bring to the attention of a union representative or committee, which then seeks to correct it with the company. In the 1930s and 1940s these would often be dealt with and resolved through militant job actions (a brief strike known as a "quickie"); in later years more laborious grievance procedures were established to deal with such matters.

ideology—a set of ideas or a belief system utilized to make sense of reality.

incentive pay—a system of payment based on the amount of production turned out by workers.

indentured servant—someone subjected to a form of temporary slavery which bound impoverished European laborers in colonial North

America to their master for a fixed period of time (between four and seven years) in exchange for a lump sum (often the price of transportation from Europe, a small parcel of forestland, and some household belongings).

industrial capitalism—a form of capitalism that is essentially based on producing goods through the factory system.

industrial democracy—a phrase once used to describe unions as a humanizing force at the workplace, sometimes having radical implications about establishing democratic control over the industrial economy.

Industrial Revolution—the major economic shift from muscle power to machine power, with great advances in technology in the late eighteenth and early nineteenth centuries turning capitalist countries in Europe and America into mass-production economies characterized by rising productivity, dramatic increases in wealth, and intensified global expansion.

industrial union—a union which includes all workers in a particular industry or workplace regardless of their specific occupation or skill.

Industrial Workers of the World—a radical industrial union organized in 1905, which sought to enroll all workers in militant struggles to improve their wages and conditions at the workplace as part of a strategy to end capitalism and place the economy under workers' control.

inflation—rising prices, which means that a dollar buys less than it used to. Some have argued that it is caused by greedy workers demanding pay increases. But inflation often increases even when workers' pay does not increase. Labor radicals call for a universally imposed escalator clause as a means to defeat inflation (while acknowledging that this may be detrimental to profits of businesses).

injunction—an order by a judge not to do something (such as picketing by a union).

international union—a union with members in more than one country; many U.S. unions that also have members in Canada are called "international unions."

IWW—Industrial Workers of the World.

Jim Crow—another word for racial segregation that places African Americans in a separate and subordinate position in relation to whites. ("Jim Crow" was a stereotyped, presumably comical African American character in racist "minstrel shows" that were popular among many nineteenth-century whites in the United States.) In the labor movement in the late nineteenth and early to mid-twentieth centuries, many union locals, especially in the AFL, refused admittance to black members but in some cases allowed the creation of "Jim Crow" locals for blacks that might be taken into the union.

journeyman—a skilled worker who has served a training period (as an apprentice) to learn his craft and is now fully qualified.

jurisdiction—involving which union has the right to represent which particular workers; failure of competing unions to agree on this results in jurisdictional disputes.

Knights of Labor—a large and inclusive organization of working people founded in 1869, first as a secret group but later as a very open and public one, which included within its purview various trade union, social, cultural, educational, and reform activities. Was most influential in the 1880s.

labor—referring to work, which is essential for the production of goods and services as well as for the acquiring of wages or salaries in our present economy, it is more generally essential for the creation of what people need to live, and is (with nature) the source of wealth. It also refers to the labor movement, and sometimes to the working class as a whole.

Labor Day—a holiday in celebration of the labor movement first initiated by labor radicals such as P. J. McGuire in New York City on September 5, 1882.

labor movement—refers to the organizations and struggles of the working class. In many countries this includes unions, political parties, consumer cooperatives, publications, clubs, and various other entities. In the United States it has often been understood more narrowly as simply "unions."

labor party—a self-consciously working-class political party, largely based in the unions and other working-class organizations.

Landrum-Griffin Act—the Labor-Management Reporting and Disclosure Act of 1959, containing regulations for union election procedures and government supervision of their financial affairs. Initiated in the wake of government investigations of racketeering in the labor movement, although seen by many as extending dangerous precedents of government interference in union activities.

laissez-faire—French term meaning "leave alone," referring to an economic policy which would prevent government from attempting to regulate business or develop social programs to help workers or the poor. According to partisans of laissez-faire capitalism, if the economy is controlled by profit-minded businessmen free from government interference, prosperity will result and benefits will trickle down to all.

left-wing—having to do with people, groups, ideas, etc., representing a radical form of "rule by the people," generally anticapitalist and favoring popular control over the economy; includes socialists, communists, anarchists.

liberal—favoring a constitutional republic with civil liberties (freedom of expression), by the late nineteenth century also favoring political democracy, while at the same time embracing capitalism; nineteenth-century liberals (and today's so-called neoliberals, also similar to "neoconservatives") favor laissez-faire policies, while most twentieth-century liberals have favored some government regulation of the economy with social programs to aid the disadvantaged.

local union—a basic organizational unit of a union, representing all union members in a particular workplace or (in the case of some craft unions) in a particular city.

lockout—when an employer shuts down the workplace to force the workers (by "locking them out") to meet his demands.

Marxism—a radical and socialist orientation that has had considerable influence in the labor movement, associated with the theories and perspectives of Karl Marx. Marxism includes five basic components:

(1) a philosophical approach sometimes called dialectical materialism; (2) a theory of history giving stress to economic development and class struggle; (3) a critical analysis of capitalism; (4) a program for the labor movement that calls for building trade unions and labor parties and for reform struggles that lead to the workers taking political power; and (5) a vision of a socialist society to be initiated once the workers establish their political rule.

mass production—production in large quantities, through the employment of many workers and the utilization of substantial technology.

master—the master craftsman was the boss in skilled handicraft shops of the eighteenth and early nineteenth century, a former journeyman who now owned a small shop where he employed several journeymen and perhaps some apprentices to work with him; on a plantation in the pre–Civil War South, a master was the owner of slaves.

May Day—May 1, 1886 saw nationwide strikes and demonstrations for the 8-hour day, initiated by P. J. McGuire and others through the predecessor of the AFL. In 1889 the international socialist movement proclaimed this an international workers' holiday, which it remains in many countries.

mechanic—another word for a skilled craftsman; often a skilled worker who works on machinery.

mediation—attempts by an impartial third party to get workers and management to make an agreement that will resolve a dispute.

mercantile—commercial; having to do with buying and selling

mercantilism—an economic policy, predominant in the seventeenth and eighteenth centuries, involving government regulation of trade and other economic activity to ensure the general welfare of the society (as defined by a king and his advisors).

merchant-capitalist—a businessman who concentrated on buying and selling (as opposed to manufacturing) commodities. He might buy raw materials, distribute them to workers in small shops or homes who would make products; then he would gather up the finished products (after paying a wage) and market them to retail stores.

middle class—a rather loose, fuzzy concept that can mean very different things, depending on the context. The "middle classes" in the sixteenth, seventeenth, and eighteenth centuries (and even in the nineteenth century in some countries) were prosperous "commoners" directly below the upper class of hereditary nobles or aristocrats. This middle layer, which secured its income through the "buying and selling" economy of capitalism, was made up of businessmen and well-to-do professionals (doctors, lawyers, etc.) who in France were called *bourgeois*—but after the obliteration of the aristocracy, most in this onetime middle layer now constitute an *upper* class. In some contexts the "middle class" later referred to small business people, shopkeepers, self-employed artisans and craftsmen, etc. Sometimes it has been used to refer to white-collar workers such as teachers, writers and journalists, government employees, clerical workers, sales employees, etc. Sometimes it refers to the bulk of the employed working class (whether blue-collar or white-collar), those who are neither rich nor poor but have a "middle income."

militant—spirited, vigorous, uncompromising. (Often wrongly defined as the same as military activity or violent activity.)

mill—factory.

mine—site of extractive industry producing coal, iron, copper, silver, gold, etc.

minimum wage—the lowest wage an employer is allowed to pay by law or union contract.

National Labor Relations Act—passed in 1935 under the sponsorship of Senator Robert Wagner of New York, representing a fundamental government shift supportive of (while establishing certain controls over) unions. It created a National Labor Relations Board to guarantee the right of workers to form unions of their own choosing, to establish the union's authority with the employer if a majority of workers vote for it through a supervised election, and to bargain effectively with employers. Modified by the Taft-Hartley Act of 1947.

National Labor Union—first effort, in 1866, to establish a nationwide federation of trade unions and other organizations of workers.

national union—a combination of local unions of a particular craft or industry (or set of more or less related occupations) all over the country.

nativism—hostility toward immigrants and others considered impure; generally involves racial and/or ethnic bigotry.

New Deal—sweeping social reforms, programs, and policies initiated by President Franklin D. Roosevelt in the 1930s, largely to aid working people, the unemployed, and others who were economically disadvantaged during the Great Depression.

no-strike pledge—a promise made by unions that they will not strike, generally given during wartime.

Occupational Safety Health Act (OSHA)—passed in 1970, authorizing the Secretary of Labor to establish and enforce health and safety standards in workplaces. Employer resistance and insufficient funding have hampered its implementation.

open shop—a business that—in contrast to both a union shop and a closed shop—employs workers regardless of union membership. This is a device to prevent unions from securing the right to represent the workers at that workplace.

overtime—working more than the number of normal hours set by law or union contract. Workers on overtime often receive a higher rate of pay. Sometimes they don't have the right to refuse overtime (forced overtime). It is argued by some that overtime contributes to unemployment.

paternalism—when an authority, often an employer, considers itself the "father" of those under it, offering them benefits while seeking to regulate their lives.

pension—a regular sum of money paid to sustain a retired employee.

picketing—what workers do when they go out on strike or are locked out: walking back and forth in front of the workplace carrying signs that tell what the dispute is about, seeking to discourage nonstriking workers, scabs, and customers from entering. Mass picketing proved most effective (but has been severely limited since the late 1940s, with the passage of Taft-Hartley Act and other antilabor laws). Milder informational picketing is also utilized in non-strike situations.

piecework—instead of being paid an hourly rate, a worker is paid by the individual piece worked on or completed. Designed to force the worker to work harder and faster.

Pinkertons—agents of the Allan Pinkerton Detective Agency hired by employers throughout the country in the late nineteenth century to act as company spies in unions and to break strikes, often through force and violence. There were other strike-breaking outfits (the Burns Detective Agency, Bergoff Industrial Service, etc.), sometimes amounting to small private armies, operating widely in the United States until the late 1930s. (Sometimes local and state police or state militias performed similar functions, later causing the Pinkerton Detective Agency to shift its operations.)

plant—factory.

political action—efforts to bring about social reforms, to pressure public officials by protesting injustices, to force or block the passage of laws, to influence elections, to bring about changes in government and social policies, etc. Especially since the 1930s, U.S. unions often focused on electoral support for political candidates and lobbying Democrats and Republicans. In some countries labor electoral efforts have been geared to advance working-class parties (labor parties, socialist parties, etc.).

politics—activities having to do with the rules, institutions, and decision making that govern society. This can include deliberations within a congress or parliament, electoral campaigns and voting, referendums, lobbying, street-corner agitation for reforms, petitioning, leafleting and other public educational efforts, rallies and demonstrations, and sit-ins and other nonviolent civil disobedience. It also could include such different activities as a military coup to set up a repressive dictatorship or a mass revolution to give "power to the people." Often economic issues and activities are also political—such as a corporation funding political candidates or seeking to break a union, or a union agitating for new laws or conducting a strike.

popular culture—a development in modern society, especially since the Industrial Revolution, involving a variety of creative activities and forms of entertainment that have mass appeal and that are related in complex ways to a consumer economy. Aspects of *popular culture* include music, art, movies, novels and short stories, radio, television, comic strips and comic books, sports, dance, amusement parks, video and computer games, etc. According to cultural historian Jim Cullen, *"popular culture* depends on the existence of a modern working class to use it, as well as to play a pivotal role in creating it."

private enterprise—capitalism.

productivity—a measure of efficiency in production, generally involving the production of more goods with the same or less labor-time.

profit—the amount of surplus made by a businessman from the sale of his business's product, over and above the cost of labor, machinery, raw materials, etc. There are fierce controversies over what is a "fair" profit. The dynamics of the market generally cause businessmen to seek maximum profits. Many business defenders argue that profits are the necessary incentives that provide for dynamism and growth of the economy, and that businessmen deserve all the profits they can get for the services they perform and the risks they take in organizing and running the economy. Labor radicals argue that since labor is the source of all profits, all profits are necessarily the result of exploitation.

progress—change for the better. Some changes are better for some people than for others. Sometimes industrial progress has had devastating consequences for millions of people. The progress represented by the labor movement has often been denounced as detrimental to the progress desired by businessmen (and vice versa).

prosperity—economic "good times" when there is economic growth, business is good, and almost everyone is able to find employment.

protectionism—the utilization of high tariffs to protect industry in one's own country from competition of industries in other countries.

pure and simple unionism—a form of unionism which focuses on pushing for improved wages, hours, and working conditions at the workplace, tending to accept capitalism as a given and shying away from larger visions of radical social reform or revolutionary change.

quickie—a brief work stoppage in a workplace, initiated by workers to force management to back off from an unpopular policy or to quickly resolve a grievance in the interests of the workers.

race—a concept developed after the 1400s, in large measure to set up hierarchies of "superior" and "inferior" peoples in an age of European expansion and global conquest, and which also had impact on the consciousness and practices of different sectors of the U.S. working class. Often used as a synonym for what are now labeled ethnic groups, race was even more commonly utilized to create a category of "whiteness" through which people with European origins attained certain rights and benefits that set them above those with African, Asian, or Native American ("Indian") origins. Scientifically, race can be defined as a biological grouping within the human species classified according to specific genetically inherited differences such as skin pigmentation, hair texture and color, body proportions, etc. (or more precisely measurable differences in blood type, amino acid excretions, and enzyme deficiencies). Yet such races are in a continual state of flux, with genes constantly flowing from one gene pool to another, and since all racial groups currently existing are consequently thoroughly mixed, there is significant variation in racial classification systems. Some scientists have identified three races (Mongoloid, Caucasoid, Negroid), others refer to five, yet others referring to more than thirty—some listing over two hundred, and yet others questioning the value of racial categories altogether. Much use of the term "race" is biologically and scientifically meaningless, being an ideological construction (at best loosely related to scientific notions) utilized to explain or justify differences, conflicts and inequalities that are actually rooted in cultural and socioeconomic developments. What places someone in a specific race is often illogical: there are dark-skinned "whites" with darker complexions than light-skinned "blacks"; the child of a black mother and a white father is considered black, yet the child of a white mother and a black father is also considered black; etc. Nonetheless, race has a genuine social meaning, since most people consider themselves (and are considered by others) to be in one or another distinct race, and this is deeply rooted in the historical experience and consciousness of the U.S. working class—creating perhaps the sharpest and most damaging division in the ranks of labor.

racism—negative attitudes, practices, and policies directed at people because of their race or ethnic background.

racketeering—making money through shady or illegal means.

radical—often meaning "extreme," but more accurately meaning "going to the root" of a problem and favoring far-reaching solutions; often synonymous with someone or something *left-wing*.

raiding—a common practice among competing unions, in which one union seeks to increase its membership not by organizing non-unionized workers, but at the expense of another union, by persuading employees in a unionized workplace to replace the rival union with one's own.

rank and file—the membership or social base of an organization, socioeconomic class, or nation, exclusive of its leaders.

real wages—wages expressed in terms of what today's dollar will buy, often based on the Consumer Price Index. It is possible that you are making more dollars in your paycheck now than was the case five years ago, but that your paycheck now will buy fewer goods—in which case your real wages have decreased.

recession—mild depression or slowdown in economic growth, with rise in unemployment.

red—associated with left-wing views; during the cold war associated with Communism.

red-baiting—seeking to discredit someone or something by charging that they are left-wing or Communistic.

reform—a change designed to bring improvement.

reformer—someone who advocates and works for reforms.

reformist—someone who believes that the ills of society can gradually be eliminated simply through the accumulation of reforms.

replacement worker—polite term for a scab who takes someone else's job during a strike.

republic—government by elected representatives (posing the question as to who actually elects the representatives—that is, whether the republic is democratic or elitist).

revolutionary—involving a dramatic change in fundamental political and economic power relations. Often this is associated with violent change, although there have been nonviolent revolutionaries.

right-to-work laws—a term used by opponents of unions to establish open-shop laws. The term has nothing to do with guaranteeing anyone the right to a job.

right-wing—having to do with people, groups, ideas, etc—including those labeled conservative—that are in opposition to radical-democratic currents or the orientations of socialists, communists, anarchists, etc.

robber barons—a derogatory term for businessmen who made fortunes in the post–Civil War period, presumably by unethical means; referred to more positively by some as "captains of industry."

robotics—self-correcting feedback and computer electronics guiding machinery, replacing human workers; similar to automation.

runaway shops—factories and other business enterprises that move away from unionized and higher-wage areas to non-union and low-wage areas.

salary—a form of pay for labor, generally paid monthly or semimonthly, especially to clerical and professional workers (rather than manual workers); it was commonly perceived as reflecting status a step "above" the traditional (blue-collar) working class—although this notion had worn thin by the late twentieth century.

scab—someone who takes someone else's job during a strike.

secondary boycott—if there is a strike or lockout at one plant and the employer sends out work to another plant, and the workers at the second plant refuse to do that work in solidarity with the striking or locked-out workers, their refusal is a secondary boycott.

seniority—a workers' length of service with an employer. According to most union contracts, a worker with greater seniority is laid off later and called back to work sooner than a worker with less seniority; often there are other benefits as well, involving the right to be promoted to a better job at a workplace, higher pay rates, more vacation time, etc. The seniority system was developed by unions to eliminate arbitrary penalization of workers (often for union activity) and to promote a system of fairness and relative worker security at the workplace.

service worker—a very elastic term, involving employees (of a variety of skill, status, income levels) in service occupation as opposed to manufacturing or agricultural occupations.

sexism—negative attitudes, practices, and policies directed at people because of their sex or gender (females generally being the direct victims of this).

sit-down strike—a strike in which the workers occupy the factory instead of leaving it, placing greater pressure on the employer because it is consequently impossible to get production going with scab labor, and repressive violence directed against the strikers could damage expensive machinery and other valued property of the employer. A highly effective tactic that was common in the 1930s but which diminished when employers sought to be less intransigent, labor leaders sought to be more respectable, and laws made it more difficult to sustain militant union confrontations.

shop—workplace.

shop steward—a union representative in the workplace whom workers can consult immediately if they face a problem with the employer or management, and who ensures that the union is a living presence in union members' daily work lives.

skilled worker—a worker needing a significant amount of training and experience (such as a carpenter, an electrician, a tool-and-die maker, etc.).

slavery—a system of forced labor. The laborer is forced to work for someone else (often known as the master) in order to produce enough to sustain both slave and master. In some slave systems the slave has certain rights and can look forward to being set free eventually. Under the system sometimes termed *chattel slavery* (chattel means movable property) in the U.S. South, which was ended by the Civil War of 1861–1865, the slaves were the permanent property of a master, generally with no more rights than farm animals: they could be bought and sold, used for breeding more slaves, separated from loved ones, "disciplined" through force and violence, abused in multiple ways, or sometimes even killed. Some have referred to the general situation of the working class as wage slavery: workers are forced—if they wish to make a living (purchase what they need to live)—to sell their ability to labor to the employer for a certain number of hours; the employer owns that essential part of their lives, and seeks to control as much of their lives as possible in order to squeeze as much actual labor out of the investment as possible; the worker is not property (only the sold portions of his or her labor-power belong to the employer), but the worker does support himself or herself (and sometimes a family) *plus the employer* through this forced labor— yet also struggles to secure as much freedom (self-determination, control over one's own life) as possible.

slowdown—slowing down by workers of the pace of work, and therefore the amount of output—usually used as a tactic to pressure employers to shift away from policies or practices that the workers object to.

social unionism—an approach which involves unions not only being concerned about immediate objectives (improvements in wages, hours, working conditions) but also seeking to reform social conditions in order to better the general society.

socialism—a perspective that the economy should be socially owned (by all in society), democratically controlled, and utilized through humanistic planning to benefit all people. It has sometimes been synonymous with "communism," but sometimes a distinction has been made between the two—especially since the 1917 Russian revolution. The popular conception of socialism does not as often have the undemocratic connotation that is associated with the Communism of the dictator Stalin and his imitators and successors. There are different currents of socialist thought—some but not all influenced by Marxism, some revolutionary and some reformist.

Social Security—a New Deal reform which involved workers and employers paying a tax to the federal government in order to provide social security payments, a type of pension, to retired employees.

society—system of human organization for large-scale community living that normally furnishes protection, security, and identity for its members. Modern societies generally involve complex economies and political dynamics, and are influenced by divisions based on class.

solidarity—a strong feeling of unity or fellowship (brotherhood and sisterhood) based on common interests flowing from being part of the same group or class.

speedup—a common complaint by workers describing company attempts to speed up the pace of work in order to increase production, generally without an increase in pay.

stool pigeon—someone paid by employers or others to infiltrate a labor organization and report on its activities.

strike—a temporary halt in work by all the workers together, in order to pressure the employer to improve their conditions. A strike is generally run by the union and involves workers picketing at the entrances of their workplace.

sweetheart contract—a contract between a corrupt union and an employer (often negotiated behind the backs of the workers) which brings benefits to employers and union officials but not to the union membership.

sympathy strike—a strike by workers not directly involved in a labor dispute to show solidarity with the initial strikers and increase pressure on their employer. If extended broadly enough, this becomes a general strike.

Taft-Hartley Act—adopted in 1947 to limit the power and eliminate radicalism of unions. It outlaws the closed shop, jurisdictional strikes, secondary boycotts, sympathy strikes; reinstates the injunction to limit other boycotts and strike activity; imposes "cooling-off" periods before strikes can be called; provides for limitations on picketing, prevents unions from directly contributing to electoral campaigns, and requires all union officers to file affidavits that they are not members of the Communist Party. States were allowed to enact anti-union "right to work" laws. Unions were required to submit their constitutions, bylaws, and financial statements to the U.S. Department of Labor. Unions not complying with all of this would be denied the protections of the National Labor Relations Act and the services of the National Labor Relations Board.

tariff—a tax placed on foreign goods in order to make the foreign imports more expensive than similar goods produced inside the country (which are consequently easier to sell). A high tariff policy is called "protectionism."

technology—tools; branch of knowledge dealing with industrial arts, applied science, engineering, etc. The development of technology increases productivity, cutting down on the amount of labor needed to create a product, at the same time creating more goods for society (sometimes called a greater social surplus) that can be utilized to advance general human development and/or to increase individual wealth.

tenant farmer—also known as a sharecropper who—after the breakup of the slave system on Southern plantations after the Civil War—rented farmland and was compelled to give roughly a third of the crop for the profit of the landowner and at least another third of the crop to pay for provisions, tools, and other necessities.

trade union—generally a synonym for "union," whether organized along craft or industrial lines. (Sometimes understood more narrowly as referring simply to craft unions.)

unemployment compensation—payments made to jobless workers by the government, funded by a tax paid by the employee to cover such payments.

unfair labor practices—defined by (and prohibited by) the National Labor Relations Act and Taft-Hartley Act as practices of discrimination, coercion, and intimidation by management or unions. Management is prohibited from setting up company unions or using coercive tactics to discourage union organization. Unions are not to force workers to join organizations not of their own choosing.

union—an organization of workers in a workplace or trade or industry which seeks to raise wages, shorten the workday, improve working conditions, establish dignity on the job. The word comes from the Latin word *unus*, meaning "one." The union consists of all the union members, and "an injury to one is an injury to all."

union contract—a written agreement between a union and an employer. It lists wages, hours, conditions of employment, and various rights and responsibilities that have been agreed to.

union label—a stamp or tag on products to show that the work was done by union labor.

union shop—a workplace where every member of the bargaining unit must become a member of the union after a specified amount of time.

unorganized worker—a worker who does not belong to a union.

unskilled worker—a worker who can be trained for a job in a few days or weeks.

wages—a form of pay for labor, often set at an hourly rate (though sometimes by the piece of work done) and generally paid daily or weekly for manual (blue-collar) labor.

wages system—an economic system based on workers selling their ability to work for regular payment (the wage) to an employer who has control over the economy; usually understood to be capitalism.

Wagner Act—the National Labor Relations Act of 1935, generally seen as a pro-labor law that, with government protections and involvement, made it much easier for unions to organize and operate. It was modified by the Taft-Hartley Act which had the opposite effect.

welfare capitalism—associated with paternalistic policies developed by employers especially in the 1920s, designed to provide various company benefits to employees in order to discourage unionization and to develop worker loyalty to the company.

welfare state—a term which gained currency after World War II, generally referring to capitalist countries in which a wide range of social benefits are provided by the government—such as unemployment compensation, social security payments to the elderly and disabled, health insurance, aid to education, low-income housing.

white-collar worker—worker not required to do heavy physical labor, such as office workers, retail clerks, teachers—as opposed to those having factory, farm, and construction jobs.

wildcat strike—a strike of the workers, often spontaneous, which is not authorized by the union.

Wobbly—nickname for a member of the revolutionary union the IWW. One anecdote claims that its origin was with a Chinese immigrant worker who had just joined it and had difficulty pronouncing the letter W, therefore saying that he had just become a member of the "I-Wobbly-Wobbly."

workers compensation—insurance payments, provided by all states, received when a worker is injured on the job.

working class—includes employed people and their family members whose living is dependent on selling labor-power (the ability to work) to employers for wages or salaries, plus underemployed or unemployed sectors unable to secure such living wages or salaries (therefore dependent on unemployment compensation, welfare benefits, etc.), and those former wage and salary workers who have reached retirement age.

yellow dog contract—a statement workers were forced to sign, as a basis for getting a job, promising that they would not join a union. Sometimes known as an "iron-clad oath."

Timeline of the
History of the United States

1775	American Revolution, 1775–1783
1780	
1785	
1790	
1795	
1800	
1805	
1810	
1815	
1820	Industrial Revolution comes to U.S., 1820s
1825	
1830	
1835	
1840	
1845	Mexican War, 1846–1848
1850	
1855	
1860	Civil War, 1861–1865
1865	
1870	
1875	
1880	
1885	Populist revolt develops among farmers
1890	
1895	Spanish-American War, 1898
1900	Progressive Era, social reforms; radical workers struggles
1905	
1910	NAACP founded, 1909
1915	
1920	U.S. enters World War I, 1917–1918
	Conservative, "Prosperous" 1920s (but 40% of people live at poverty level)
1925	
1930	Great Depression (mass unemployment & poverty), radical workers struggles, 1929
1935	New Deal (social reforms), 1933–1939
1940	
1945	U.S. enters World War II, 1941–1945
	anti-Communist Cold War begins, 1946–47
1950	1950s–1960s—widespread prosperity, Civil Rights movement
1955	
1960	1960s—U.S. War on Poverty launched, U.S. War in Vietnam escalates (both fail);
1965	widespread protests
1970	
1975	
1980	1980s—Reagan "Revolution" (cutbacks or social programs,
1985	decline of industry & good-paying jobs, growing inequality)
1990	

immigration from Europe; "first wave" majority from Germany & Ireland

slave trade, slavery; antislavery struggle

WESTWARD EXPANSION

pushing back, fighting, destroying Native American ("Indian") peoples

closing of the Frontier

immigration from Europe— "second wave" majority from southern & eastern Europe

World War I and anti-immigrant laws cut flow of immigration

upsurge of KKK attacks on blacks & immigrants

Great Northward Migration of African Americans

Reconstruction (pro-black), 1866–77; betrayal of Reconstruction; KKK-type racist violence; segregation laws; white supremacist regimes in South

The rise of the United States as a powerful industrial economy and the rise of big business corporations that dominate the U.S. economy

U.S. Labor History Chronology

1492   Christopher Columbus lands in America, beginning a European invasion which has a devastating impact upon the native inhabitants and laborers who are called mistakenly "Indians." In coming years many are enslaved to labor in mines, plantations, etc., of the newcomers, and many initiate five centuries of resistance.

1619   First African slaves are brought to the Virginia colony.

1676   Bacons' Rebellion of indentured servants, slaves, and poor colonists against the well-to-do privileged elements governing the Virginia colony.

1765   The Sons of Liberty and other radical social-protest groups, made up largely of artisans, craftsmen, and laborers, are formed to protest against what they consider to be unfair policies associated with British rule (including taxation without representation).

1770   A working-class crowd comes into conflict with British soldiers in Boston, resulting in the Boston Massacre, in which five protestors are killed. The incident further radicalizes the colonial protests.

1773   A crowd of mechanics, laborers, and other members of the Sons of Liberty dress as Indians and throw tea from the British monopoly, the East India Tea Company, into Boston's harbor, escalating the confrontation between Britain and her North American colonies.

1776   The Declaration of Independence declares the creation of the United States, based on revolutionary and democratic principles.

1778   Journeymen printers combine to increase their wages.

1786   Three years after the revolutionary victory, conflicts between poor farmers and laborers and well-to-do business elements generate such varied conflicts as Shays rebellion in Massachusetts and a militant printers' strike in Philadelphia.

1789   The U.S. Constitution is adopted, establishing a strong central government and consolidating the institution of slavery.

1791   Because of strong popular pressures, especially from working people, the Bill of Rights is added to the Constitution. Philadelphia carpenters carry out the first strike in the building trades, seeking—unsuccessfully—to establish a ten-hour workday.

1792   First local union organized for collective bargaining established by Philadelphia shoemakers.

1807   Unions are judged to be criminal conspiracies at the trial of Philadelphia shoe workers.

1820s   Industrial Revolution takes hold in the United States. This helps to set the stage for conflict between the free labor system of the North with the slave labor system of the South (contributing to a growing movement in the North for the abolition of slavery). It also generates growing organization of unions and reform groups among Northern workers.

1822   Denmark Vesey (a free black carpenter) organizes an ill-fated slave revolt in Charleston, South Carolina.

1825   A trade-union organization of women workers, the United Tailoresses of New York, is formed.

1827   Philadelphia workers band together to agitate for the ten-hour workday.

1828   The Workingmen's Party is formed in Philadelphia, and similar parties soon spread to other states, advocating extensive rights for workers, free public education, and abolition of imprisonment for debt.

1831   Nat Turner's slave rebellion in Virginia, quickly defeated, leads to repressive policies.

1837   An economic depression, known as the Panic of 1837, destroys a growing labor movement.

1840   Workers in Philadelphia strike for and win the ten-hour workday. A ten-hour workday is established for federal employees.

1842   Massachusetts Supreme Court decides that trade unions are not illegal conspiracies. Massachusetts and Connecticut pass laws prohibiting children from working more than ten hours a day.

1846–1848   Mexican War, largely generated by proslavery forces in the United States, results in the acquisition from Mexico of a large chunk of new territory (much of it potentially to be slave states), also incorporating a significant number of Mexican Americans into the U.S. workforce.

1850s   Economic growth generates the development of national unions among those who are part of the "free labor" system. At the same time, dramatic developments having to do with the slave labor system include the 1850 passage of a severe Fugitive Slave Act and the 1857 Dred Scott Decision in which the Supreme Court declared that African Americans are not entitled to citizenship rights. On the other hand, Harriet Beecher Stowe's novel *Uncle Tom's Cabin* contributes to the antislavery cause, armed conflict prevents a proslavery victory in Kansas, and an antislavery raid in Harpers Ferry, Virginia by John Brown is defeated but brings the country closer to civil war.

1852   Typographical Union formed—the first durable national organization of workers.

1861   Civil war breaks out when a majority of the slave states break away from the United States after the election of Abraham Lincoln.

1863   With the Emancipation Proclamation, the struggle against slavery officially becomes a central issue in the U.S. struggle against the slave states. With the Gettysburg Address, Lincoln also emphasizes the centrality of the radical-democratic ideals first expressed in the Declaration of Independence.

1865   The Civil War ends with a victory for a unified United States and the abolition of slavery. Industrial development of the U.S. economy, under the control of big business corporations, quickly accelerates. Within twenty-five years the United States becomes the world's leading manufacturing nation—but there is to be much resentment against the industrial and financial "robber barons."

1866   National Labor Union is organized by labor and reform groups. In the South efforts begin to initiate a radical Reconstruction that will result in the ascendancy of black and white poor laborers over the previous ruling class of wealthy plantation owners.

1869   The Knights of Labor is founded, with men and women of "every craft, creed and color" to be accepted into membership. Radical Reconstruction in the South begins to stall because dominant political and economic forces in the North fear going "too far" in challenging the property rights of the old Southern ruling class.

1873   The labor movement loses much of its momentum when a severe depression causes widespread unemployment. Highly organized white racist terrorism in the South increasingly pushes back Reconstruction forces there. Repression of Molly Maguires in eastern Pennsylvania coal regions.

1874   First use of union label, by Cigar Makers International Union.

1877   Railroad workers protesting wage cuts initiate a mass strike movement throughout much of the country, which draws many thousands of workers into militant and sometimes violent conflict with employers and government authorities. The strike is brutally repressed. Reconstruction is officially ended as compromise stuck between upper classes and politicians in North and South—with "white power" secured by organized violence and later by racist "Jim Crow" segregation laws.

1881   A number of craft unions form the Federation of Organized Trades and Labor Unions (predecessor of the AFL) under the leadership of labor radicals moving toward a "pure and simple" union approach.

1882   On the first Monday of September, the first Labor Day parade takes place in New York City. In California white workers organize at the expense of Chinese immigrant workers who are the target of their racist protests.

1884   The Bureau of Labor is established. It later grows into the U.S. Department of Labor, formally established in 1913.

1886   Nationwide agitation for the eight-hour workday culminates in massive strikes and demonstrations on May 1 (the first May Day). Radical labor leaders in Chicago are targeted for victimization (and eventual hanging) after police and worker deaths result from police suppression of the Haymarket Square rally. American Federation of Labor formed, seeking to establish union movement on more secure organizational footing.

1887   Flurry of labor party activity in various cities, especially pronounced in Chicago and New York City (where United Labor Party mayoral candidate Henry George almost wins).

1892   Near Pittsburgh, employees at the Homestead steelworks owned by Andrew Carnegie resist a concerted effort to break their strong union, successfully defeating Pinkertons and scabs in a pitched battle. State militia enters to break the strike.

1894   Pullman railroad-car workers secure support from the American Railway Union led by Eugene V. Debs in their struggle against wage cuts. A very effective strike is smashed by government injunction and federal troops. Ironically, this government strikebreaking takes place within the same period that Labor Day is set as a national holiday.

Early 1900s   Beginning of the Progressive era, in which many reform struggles were initiated. The formation of Socialist Party of America (1901), the Women's Trade Union League (1904), the Niagara Movement (1905—immediate predecessor of the National Association for the Advancement of Colored People created in 1909), and many other such groups helped to push "mainstream" politics in the direction of addressing multifaceted working-class concerns.

1905   Industrial Workers of the World is formed by labor radicals who believe in the need for an industrial union with a revolutionary orientation to overthrow the wages system. The IWW becomes a beacon of militant and all-inclusive unionism, although its hopes for an eventual nationwide general strike never materialize.

1909   The "rising of the twenty thousand" among predominantly female garment workers sweeps through New York City.

1911   The Triangle Fire in New York City's garment district results in the death of 154 workers, mostly young women. The resulting outcry generates the first serious workplace safety laws.

1912   The Lawrence, Massachusetts textile strike led by the IWW symbolizes the ability of immigrant workers from diverse backgrounds to stand together. Emphasizing that they want more than simply economic gains, the strikers—men, women, children—rally to the slogan of "Bread and Roses."

1914   Striking miners and their families in Ludlow, Colorado are machine-gunned by state militia. After the Ludlow Massacre, in which thirty-nine men, women, and children died, insurgent miners counterattack and rout the militia—only to be defeated by federal troops sent in by President Wilson.

1917   U.S. entry into World War I generates opposition by radical labor currents, which are suppressed, but more moderate trade unionists of the AFL support the war effort and are able to secure widespread union recognition and gains.

1919   Massive and militant postwar labor upsurge. Great steel strike, coal strikes, textile strikes, Boston police strike, Seattle general strike, and other events shake the country—but are savagely repressed. Large-scale government raids and arrests, coordinated by U.S. Attorney-General A. Mitchell Palmer, hit the IWW and other radical labor groups.

1920   Employers launch "the American Plan" to combat unions.

1924   Unions (including AFL), farmers groups, radicals and others attempt to launch a Conference for Progressive Political Action with a presidential campaign organized around Robert M. La Follette—though with disappointing results for many of its supporters.

1925   Brotherhood of Sleeping Car Porters founded by A. Philip Randolph and others.

1926   Government passes the Railway Labor Act, establishing collective bargaining in that industry.

1929   Great Depression begins, with unprecedented business failures and unemployment.

1932   Norris-LaGuardia Act restricts injunctions against strik-
            ers and outlaws yellow-dog contracts.

1934   Militant general strikes in Minneapolis (centered around
            embattled teamsters), in San Francisco (centered around
            longshoremen), and Toledo (focused on Auto-lite work-
            ers) result in stunning victories—helping to launch an
            upsurge in organizing industrial unions in the mass pro-
            duction industries. Yet nationwide strikes in the cotton-
            textile industry, especially hard-fought in the South, go
            down to bitter defeat.

1935   In the AFL, several unions under the leadership of
            United Mine Workers President John L. Lewis set up a
            Committee for Industrial Organization to advance the
            cause of industrial unionism. The prolabor Wagner Act is
            passed, along with other New Deal social reforms spon-
            sored by President Franklin D. Roosevelt.

1936   Flint, Michigan sit-down strike begins, led by the CIO-
            sponsored United Auto Workers—eventually resulting in
            a resounding victory of union workers against the largest
            corporation in the United States, General Motors.

1937   Ten CIO industrial unions are expelled from the AFL.
            Memorial Day massacre in Chicago occurs when police
            fire on unarmed steelworkers and their families, killing
            ten and wounding hundreds. The CIO-sponsored Steel
            Workers Organizing Committee moves forward to organ-
            izing victories.

1938   Congress of Industrial Organizations established by
            industrial unions. A Fair Labor Standards Act is passed,
            establishing a minimum wage and abolishing child labor
            in businesses under its jurisdiction.

1940   Great Depression ends as industry is revitalized by prepa-
            rations for U.S. entry into World War II.

1941	The United States enters World War II, with the great majority of AFL and CIO unions supporting the war effort. The AFL and CIO sign a no-strike pledge for the war's duration. A. Philip Randolph heads up planning for a March on Washington to protest racist discrimination against blacks—which pressures the federal government to establish a Fair Employment Practices Committee. FEPC works to eliminate discrimination in war industries based on race, creed, or national origin.
1942	A National War Labor Board is established which pegs wage increases to rises in the cost of living. Increasing numbers of women take industrial jobs on the "home-front," and new waves of African Americans are also drawn northward to urban industrial areas by the wartime manufacturing boom.
1943	United Mine Workers challenges government's no-strike pledge when mineworkers go out on strike. "Wildcat strikes" take place in many industries to protest speedup and employer abuses.
1945–1946	The end of World War II (1945) generates a huge strike wave, with 4.5 million workers setting up picket lines throughout the country. Walter Reuther of the UAW challenges General Motors to "open the books" to prove that it cannot grant wage increases—and 200,000 autoworkers walk off the job when the company refuses. The Steelworkers, United Electrical workers, and many other unions also initiate militant and successful strike actions. The ILWU leads tough struggles of Hawaiian workers, extending democracy and workers' rights to the territory outside Honolulu.
1947	The Taft-Hartley Act is passed, beginning an antilabor offensive designed to de-radicalize, slow down, and domesticate the U.S. labor movement.
1949	CIO begins to expel so-called left-wing unions accused of being influenced by Communist Party.

1955   AFL-CIO merger takes place, with George Meany elected as its president.

1959   A national steel strike stretches out for more than a hundred days, as the United Steel Workers leads its members to victory. Following U.S. Senate investigations of racketeering in the labor movement, the Landrum-Griffin Act is passed.

1960   A landmark strike by the United Federation of Teachers in New York City secures union rights and collective bargaining for teachers. In the same period Hospital Workers Local 1199 and the American Federation of State, Country and Municipal Employees begin making dramatic breakthroughs for other service, white-collar, and public employees. Negro American Labor Council formed, headed by A. Philip Randolph.

1962   By Executive Order, the federal government recognizes the right of its employees to unionize.

1963   Initiated by the Negro American Labor Council in conjunction with other groups, major civil rights organizations, some unions, and others organize a March for Jobs and Freedom in Washington, D.C., opposing segregation and other forms of racism, and addressed by Rev. Martin Luther King Jr.

1966   United Farm Workers union led by Cesar Chavez joins the AFL-CIO. In conjunction with strikes, rallies, and marches, a UFW grape boycott involves more people in the United States than any previous effort.

1968   Martin Luther King Jr. killed while assisting sanitation workers' strike in Memphis, Tennessee. The assassination of King fails to prevent the members of American Federation of State, Country and Municipal Employees from winning a decisive victory for themselves and the cause of public employee unionization. Rise of Dodge Revolutionary Union Movement (DRUM), blending black nationalism and leftism to secure (for a short while) a significant following among black autoworkers.

1970   Postal workers strike in eight cities wins substantial victories. Hawaii and Pennsylvania pass laws giving most public employees the right to strike. Occupational Safety and Health Act passed.

1972   Coalition of Black Trade Unionists formed, reflecting the growing percentage of African Americans in the labor movement, and dedicated to overcome racism in the unions as well as in the workplace.

1974   Coalition of Labor Union Women formed, reflecting the growing percentage of women in the labor movement, and dedicated to struggle for women's rights in the unions as well as in the workplace.

1980   President Ronald Reagan begins assault on welfare-state measures that had been initiated during the New Deal era, at the same time shifting away from the labor-management "social compact" in place since the 1950s. AFL-CIO organizes a massive "Solidarity Day" march and rally in Washington, D.C.—but fails to prevent Reagan from breaking the strike and the union of Air Traffic Controllers.

1986–1987   United Food and Commercial Workers Local P-9 wages a militant strike and anticorporate campaign against the Hormel Corporation, but the power and viciousness of the company, and insufficient unity and support in the labor movement, results in defeat.

1989   The striking United Mine Workers of America demonstrates the power of militant unionism, and wins widespread labor and community support, in waging and winning an all-out battle with the Pittston Coal Company.

1992   Workers in Local 7837 of the United Paperworkers International Union launch an inspiring struggle when the A. E. Staley Manufacturing Company in Decater, Illinois, attempts to impose a twelve-hour workday on top of the steady and deadly erosion of workplace safety. A long, bitter strike is finally overwhelmed due to insufficient labor solidarity in the face of corporate power. Workers in Ravenswood, West Virginia conduct a militant strike focused on industrial safety at the Ravenswood Aluminum Company, and with powerful backing from the United Steelworkers sweep to victory.

1995   A new leadership—headed by John Sweeney, Linda Chavez-Thompson, and Richard Trumka—sweeps into the upper echelons of the AFL-CIO, proclaiming the need for a militant organizing strategy and an expansive social unionism.

1996   Two thousand workers drawn to a founding national conference of a Labor Party, whose goal is to build a base for eventual effective independent labor politics. Militant Detroit newspaper strike begins.

1997   Striking workers at United Parcel Service, led by a democratic and militant Teamsters union, win widespread public support and a stunning victory, with full-time UPS workers championing the interests of part-time workers. Pennsylvania Health Care Workers District 1199-P of SEIU finally win a hard-fought and protracted struggle to force the largest nursing home chain in the world, Beverly Enterprises, to bargain in good faith and sign a union contract. Under the banner of the United Steelworkers of America, 4,500 rubber workers at Breakstone-Firestone (in Decatur, Illinois; Des Moines, Iowa; Russellville, Arkansas; Oklahoma City, Oklahoma) conduct a month-long strike—marked by unfair labor practices from the company—which finally secures a fair contract, with the aid of a union-sponsored corporate campaign and the pressure of unfair labor practices. There is also a qualified victory for striking members of the United Steel Workers over the Wheeling-Pittsburgh Corporation in Pennsylvania, West Virginia, and Ohio—protecting endangered union pensions and blocking plant closings. Detroit newspaper strike continues, with tens of thousands rallying from various parts of the country for a solidarity march. AFL-CIO national convention prioritizes a "union cities" campaign to build a network of central labor councils that will educate, agitate, organize, and mobilize increasing sectors of the working class for improved living and working conditions and a broadly conceived "social justice" for a diverse working-class majority.

Government and politicians, business spokepeople, and some media pundits target prominent representatives of the new currents in the AFL-CIO as being "corrupt" and too powerful. Reform President Ron Carey of the Teamsters, and AFL-CIO Secretary-Treasurer Richard Trumka are accused of improperly channeling funds to reform union campaigns and Democratic Party candidates.

1998   Government overseers, in addition to forcing a new election in the Teamsters union, force the expulsion from the union of Ron Carey—enhancing the momentum of an antireform (and in some cases crime-linked) resurgence in the union spearheaded by lawyer James Hoffa Jr. and also supported by conservative Republicans. On the other hand, efforts in Congress to push through additional restrictive antilabor legislation fail.

The United Farm Workers campaign to organize strawberry workers, seemingly on the verge of success, is smashed by a powerful business counterattack—involving a violence-prone company union and skillful manipulation of California's Agricultural Labor Relations Board. Undeterred, the United Farm Workers vows to continue the struggle among strawberry workers and also intensifies organizing efforts among the state's lettuce workers.

In Puerto Rico, the island is rocked by a massive general strike initiated by the telephone workers' unions

which—despite immense enthusiasm and popular support—fail in the goal of preventing the sale of the state-
owned Puerto Rico Telephone Company to private business interests.

In Flint, Michigan almost 10,000 members of the United
Auto Workers carry out a fifty-four-day strike against
General Motors, in which widespread public support
is generated as workers battle to push back the company's demands for union "concessions" and GM plans for
"restructuring" production in order to eliminate union
jobs. While GM operations are practically shut down
nationwide and a compromise settlement achieved, the
major issues underlying the strike remain unresolved.

When 73,000 members of the Communication Workers
of America strike Bell Atlantic for three days, they succeed in blocking company efforts to eliminate union jobs
through "outsourcing" and exert pressures in opposition
to company policies of forced overtime (which compel
many workers to labor for sixty to eighty hours a week).
Additional strike action by 6,300 Connecticut telephone workers achieve pay gains and benefits for members of a former company union, the Coonecticut Union
of Telephone Workers. The Air Line Pilots Association
mobilizes 6,200 Northwest Airlines employees in a fif-
teen-day strike that secures income hikes and greater job
security—encouraging Machinists and teamsters union
workers at Northwest to pressure for similar gains. In
New York City, 40,000 construction workers stage a militant march protesting the growth of non-union firms. In
Philadelphia, a forty-day strike of the Transport Workers
Union beats back concession demands of the South
Eastern Pennsylvania Transity Authority.

The vulnerability of many workers is increased by legislation penalizing so-called illegal immigrants and pushing
through what is tagged "welfare reform." Some workers
support both measures, seeing them as helping to secure

jobs for U.S. citizens and to cut down on workers' taxes supporting alleged "welfare freeloaders." But the antiimmigrant policies make it easier for employers to compel "undocumented workers" to quietly accept highly exploitative conditions—because protests could result in deportation. And policies to "end welfare as we know it" have the effect of forcing hundreds of thousands of people into the workforce at minimum wage levels—driving down the norm in working-class living standards.

Index

About Haymarket Books

Haymarket Books is a radical, independent, nonprofit book publisher based in Chicago.

Our mission is to publish books that contribute to struggles for social and economic justice. We strive to make our books a vibrant and organic part of social movements and the education and development of a critical, engaged, international left.

We take inspiration and courage from our namesakes, the Haymarket martyrs, who gave their lives fighting for a better world. Their 1886 struggle for the eight-hour day—which gave us May Day, the international workers' holiday—reminds workers around the world that ordinary people can organize and struggle for their own liberation. These struggles continue today across the globe—struggles against oppression, exploitation, poverty, and war.

Since our founding in 2001, Haymarket Books has published more than five hundred titles. Radically independent, we seek to drive a wedge into the risk-averse world of corporate book publishing. Our authors include Noam Chomsky, Arundhati Roy, Rebecca Solnit, Angela Y. Davis, Howard Zinn, Amy Goodman, Wallace Shawn, Mike Davis, Winona LaDuke, Ilan Pappé, Richard Wolff, Dave Zirin, Keeanga-Yamahtta Taylor, Nick Turse, Dahr Jamail, David Barsamian, Elizabeth Laird, Amira Hass, Mark Steel, Avi Lewis, Naomi Klein, and Neil Davidson. We are also the trade publishers of the acclaimed Historical Materialism Book Series and of Dispatch Books.